Porn and Masculinity

The negative effect of porn on your manliness and virility

William Jackson

"When you arise in the morning think of what a privilege it is to be alive, to think, to enjoy, to love ..."

-Marcus Aurelius

CONTENTS

ACKNOWLEDGMENTS

I wish to thank my family first and foremost. My parents have always been supportive of my endeavors. Beyond them, I would like to thank all those great philosophers that lived before us. It is thanks to them that our generation has the ability to stand on the shoulders of these giants.

INTRODUCTION

We live in a world where young boys are exposed to internet porn. Where everyone is exposed to porn and imagery of sex, more than ever before. A world where men are addicted to internet porn. Men choose this pornography over interaction with real women. They prefer porn over sex with their girlfriend, and even when they are in a relationship they will refuse to surrender their porn habits. They continue their masturbatory binges. It is a world where the virtual replaces the physical. What it does not replace, and never will be able to, is that same level of satisfaction, that feeling of bliss.

What started as a monthly centerfold model in Playboy, has turned into millions of videos accessible for free on the internet. Any young boy can surf to these sites on his smartphone and become exposed to an overload of pornographic material. Often, this is their first view on sex. Some say this changes the way they treat women, and that it is damaging because it makes men overly masculine. That is not the message in this book. Porn is damaging because it makes men submissive. It does not make them overly masculine, no, it destroys their manliness.

We live in a world where feminism, talk of rape culture and the culmination of the #metoo craze has resulted in men being afraid to mentor women, men are afraid to hire women, to be alone with them. Some men do not even dare to speak sincerely to women anymore. Frankly, men are afraid to be near women, to talk to women, or to have sex with women. Oddly enough, what they are not afraid of is porn. Porn is their safe space. It is their personal on-demand fantasy world. All it takes is allowing your brain to be fooled, and to allow your passions to lead you.

Men have lost their place in the modern world. Peace has made them obsolete in their minds, as they are not aware of any purpose beyond that of a being a soldier. Now, these men are depressed, nihilistic and misguided. They understand as little of themselves as they understand of the world around them. Porn, then, becomes a place of refuge. A place that triggers their instinctual desire. A place to hide from the scary world around them. A world filled with rejection and disappointment. A world that requires effort to succeed.

We live in a world where people have fewer and fewer children. Where populations shrink; at least in the Western world, Africa is a rare exception to the rule. Where kids are seen as a financial burden, and avoided. Blessed then be pornography, as masturbation can never lead to such a result. Sex is purely for pleasure, and this pleasure can easily be obtained from porn. The desire for children has been labeled as unmanly, yet watching porn is considered a natural activity for all men. The stereotype for men is based on sitcoms that follow the likes of Al Bundy from Married with Children. It shows weak, effeminate men that have no purpose in their life. Men in sitcoms are depicted as losers. In the odd case they are not a loser, they are drunks that get into bar fights - which is really just a different type of loser.

The core male activities are now porn and video games. Any gap can be filled in with a new season of any random Netflix show. It appears that any manly activity is toxic. Even video games are attacked when they are too violent. Porn is attacked only for its extremities. Never do people talk about the harmful effect of porn in general. Porn, as a whole, is never bad, there are only certain types of porn that are bad. This book will aim to counter that belief, and show that any type of porn is damaging to whoever is watching it. The difference is merely in the extent of the damage.

And above all, we live in a world where all of this happens, without people talking about what is going on. Are these things normal? What is causing them? What is the effect? Can we change it? Our world suffers from a crisis in male identity. Men are accused of possessing toxic masculinity, they are told they need to get in touch with their superior feminine side. All that is male is bad, and men should aspire to be more like women. If only the world was ruled by women, then there would be no more wars! Or so they claim.

Men are lost in all this chaos. They are completely out of touch with their natural instincts, they do not understand them. They only know that they enjoy porn. Porn, we will show during this book, is what is misguiding men. Porn creates the worst in men, but not because it would somehow create toxic masculinity. Porn creates the worst in men, because it destroys their masculinity. Porn destroys their manliness. Porn destroys their virility.

THE RISE OF INTERNET PORN

Porn has become mainstream. The modern era has brought many new inventions that did not exist in the lives of our ancestors. The internet. Smartphones (mobile porn on its own is already a billion-dollar industry). High definition cameras. A changed sense of morality. All of these combined brought us internet porn. Accessible anywhere, anytime, for anyone. Unsurprisingly, as a society, we consume massive amounts of porn. Pornsites have more visitors than Netflix, Amazon, and Twitter combined. The porn part of total internet traffic may easily reach thirty percent. That doesn't mean that people spend thirty percent of their time online watching porn, but streaming a video takes a lot more data than browsing your Facebook newsfeed. Having said that, we could see this percentage decline over the coming years due to the rise of Netflix, but that does not mean that people are watching less porn. Whether you appreciate this or not, it would be foolish for us not to stop and think about it. Just briefly, what are the effects of this? We are performing a reckless experiment on a mass-scale. Every man is exposed to internet porn, even those that attempt to reject it from their lives will be confronted with it from time to time. Escape is near impossible. The majority of this porn that gets spread around finds its origin in the United States.

Most boys will experience internet porn by the age of ten to twelve. With the rise of smartphones, this could be even younger. By the time schools start to teach children sexual education, most children will be very familiar with sex already. They will know sex from the pornography they've seen online.

"For the first time in history, children are growing up whose earliest sexual

imprinting derives not from a living human being, or fantasies of their own; since the 1960s pornographic upsurge, the sexuality of children has begun to be shaped in response to cues that are no longer human. Nothing comparable has ever happened in the history of our species; it dislodges Freud. Today's children and young men and women have sexual identities that spiral around paper and celluloid phantoms: from Playboy to music videos to the blank females torsos in women's magazines, features obscured and eyes extinguished, they are being imprinted with a sexuality that is mass-produced, deliberately dehumanizing and inhuman."
- Naomi Wolf

The websites do attempt to block visitors that are under 18. You need to click 'yes' when prompted with the question if you are over 18, not a really foolproof system. The United Kingdom is the first country that will attempt to block access specifically to underage viewers. They will force the providers to block porn sites for all users, unless they buy a code in a physical shop where they need to show a proof of identity. This could be a drivers license or a passport. With the code they obtain, they can get access on their computer to view adult content. It is questionable how difficult it will be to bypass this law, for example by using a VPN or a leaked code, or simply by finding sites and downloads that are not covered by the adult filter, but it is a step in making it more challenging for youngsters to access such websites. That is not to say that government intervention is the way forward, as such power is easily abused for other purposes by the government, and the United Kingdom is known for its 'Big Brother' style practices. Many will also oppose this idea as it appears to be an attack on individual liberty to force adult men to obtain a license to watch porn by going to the neighborhood liquor shop. It is not necessarily a good law, but it is a law that is unique in that it recognizes the problem of excess porn consumption. Even though the law only focuses on those under 18, it still acknowledges that porn is a serious topic.

In later chapters, we will dive into specific types of porn. We will seek to understand and analyze. Yet porn there is considered merely an opening into the fantasies of the regular guy. We will discuss why certain types are popular, and what the appeal in it may be. Moreover, how does that appeal relate to the society we live in? What are the effects of watching such videos on someone's personality? Through this book, hopefully, the question of 'why is porn bad in the first place?' can be answered. There is no single answer, as everyone is different and searches for different things when they watch porn, so everyone will have a different reason for ceasing to watch porn. The goal of this book is not to make you stop watching porn, unless you recognize you are addicted to it. It will aim to make you more considerate of why your brain is pulling you towards porn and why you find it so appealing. Perhaps with such understanding of what is going on inside you, porn will lose some of its appeals. Breaking such chains may then free up your time for other uses, and ultimately improve your quality of life. By quality of life, it is meant to lead a virile life, a manly life. That is what you were made for, designed for, or evolved for, whichever you believe. Do you know how does watching porn affect our men and their manliness, their virility? Hopefully, towards the end of this book you do. In this first chapter, we will wonder what the consequences may be of near-constant exposure to the porn itself. It will introduce a few ideas that we will explore in more detail in later chapters.

Now, there are many people that can explain to you how sex in porn is different from real sex. And for those reading it that are not a virgin, you'll probably have figured this out by now. I won't go into that here. But what are the effects of relationships between men and women? Some say that men become more aggressive, that it makes them see women as pieces of meat. As in porn, they believe women are there just for sex. This sounds logical upon first hearing it, but in reality, is this what we see around us? Men have always liked women for their bodies, there is nothing new there. Therefore, pointing out that some men still value women mostly for their bodies, is not a convincing argument. Men are and have always been attracted to women that look healthy and fertile. The whole purpose of intercourse is to identify a sexual partner with those characteristics, so that they may thereby create successful offspring and a continuation of the genetic lineage. Yet today, men seem meeker when it comes to their interactions with women. Whenever men do express abuse against women, physical abuse or excessive verbal abuse, is this actually a sign of masculinity? It is a lack of self-control. It is not men that behave in such a way, but immature boys. If anything, porn is preventing men from growing up into responsible adults with an understanding of their place in the world.

Men worship porn as if it were the new God. Porn does not bring about the devaluation of women, au contraire, it brings about an absurd increase in the valuation of women. At least in the minds of these porn-consuming young men. Women are turned into something of a myth, so close within reach, yet always too far away to grasp. We can make a comparison to Tantalus. This ancient Greek was placed up to his neck in a river, with apples hanging just in front of him. Yet every time he wanted to drink, the water would lower itself beyond his reach. Every time he felt hunger and wanted to grab an apple, the branch would move away, just beyond his reach. So close, yet so far away. It is similar to young men watching porn, they are observing these attractive women so close to their reach. Yet, always just too far away for them to actually reach. Or, actually, way too far since they are only pixels on a computer screen. This creates endless frustration for millions of men around the world, a frustration that only leads to an increased desire. An increased desire, a thirst, that can never be quenched. You can't quench your thirst by shoving salt into your mouth either. Likewise, porn cannot satisfy your sexual desires, it only increases them. This Tantalus-effect is the first effect of porn that we must remember, as it drives frustration between the sexes. It makes men desperate for satisfaction, but in their desperation they try to quench their thirst by eating more and more salt. Porn changes the basic expectations of young men, and as their expectations shift, so do their desires. Since their expectations are unrealistic, based on porn, their desires can never be fulfilled.

This does not mean that there are no men that watch porn and do suddenly start to act out against women. These hypersexualized men lose all sense of reality and believe that real life is a porn scene. They may start to expose themselves to women, in the absurd belief that women secretly enjoy it and will simply start having sex with them. Workplaces may seem a suitable place for them to start hitting on every woman that walks by, up to the point of physically harassing them. It is not that no woman enjoys a workplace compliment on her looks, but it matters highly who says it and in what way. If the man giving the compliment is a man that she has secretly been interested in for a while, obviously she would appreciate the compliment. This is not the case when the compliment comes from the creepy-looking fat guy that never talked to her before.

Some men may even start to believe rape is more permissible, as they are constantly watching aggressive violent porn and the women seem to enjoy it. Such men do not understand that women's rape fantasies are always about men they already fantasize about, and that the 'rape' is never real rape, but more a symbol of a strong desire from this man. Let us be clear that this book does not condone or support any violence, either physical or verbal, against women. Despite the fact that current thinking about consent sometimes reaches the ridiculous, up to the point where it would basically require everyone to sign a contract before having sex, the fact remains that the woman obviously needs to consent to all contact. It is the porn users that see rape as less heinous of a crime compared to non-porn users. Likely, seeing women engage in casual sex on screen frequently has made these men believe that having sex is not such a big deal, and thereby they conclude that rape is a minor assault. It does not mean these men want to rape, but they are less concerned about women that do get raped. We advise manliness, not violence against women or misogyny. By all means, treat women with decency. Decency is not the same as weakness, or submissiveness.

Why is porn so attractive to watch? The effect of porn is made even greater by multiple factors that make it irresistibly appealing. One of which is the sheer attractiveness of the women featured in porn. The attractiveness adds to their mythical status, as it is beyond what these men stumble upon in their daily - real - lives. In mainstream pornography, first of all, only the more attractive looking girls are selected. The whole world is their casting ground, out of which a tiny percentage enters porn. Unattractive girls are filtered out and not shown, they need to have some form of sex appeal. Even for the 'BBW', Big Beautiful Women, categories they look for women that look attractive for their size. Mostly, they will look for girls in the prime of their lives with looks suitable for the camera.

Second, on top of that, these girls wear a considerable amount of makeup before appearing on camera. All imperfections are perfectly hidden. Their acne gets covered. They have eyelash extensions to draw more attention to their eyes. Buzzfeed has been nice enough to share 33 pictures of women that do porn with and without makeup. The differences are significant, as they look a lot more like your average neighborhood girl when their real faces are displayed. Our brains struggle to understand that it is the same person, even when the pictures are right next to one another.

Red lipstick is applied to make them look more fertile. Women make their lips red to appear more fertile and thereby more attractive to men. During ovulation, the most fertile period of the month, a woman's face is flushed with more blood. Her lips will be redder, and the same goes for her cheeks. Men's natural instinct causes them to find women with red lips more attractive. Our natural drive ensures that men are attracted to women capable of being impregnated. You could take two female identical twins, and let men rate their appearance at the same time. If one twin is on her period, while the other is ovulating, all men will rate the ovulating twin as significantly more attractive. This ovulating twin will have lips that are more red. This is despite the fact that the twins are genetically almost identical, and the results would be the complete reverse around two weeks later. Despite men being fantastic at spotting these minor differences, we only do so subconsciously.

Third, any remaining imperfections will either not be as visible on camera, or can be avoided by the angle the cameraman chooses. Scars can be made to disappear. Ugly feet can simply not be shown. You cannot smell her sweat. It only records the girls from their best angle, which is often not the same as the view the man has. And there is always a girl that looks just like the type of girl that you are looking for in that exact moment.

Porn is becoming a substitute for real life experiences for men across the world. Narcissus could not stop looking at himself, causing him to drown; but today's young men cannot stop looking at the beautiful girls they see in pornography. They end up drowning in their addiction. Real women can never compare to this level of attraction. Their imperfections are noticed. They are seen without makeup. If we would see porn models in real life, a large part of this attraction would likely fade. They would become mortals again, losing their divine status. Sadly, these young men never see these women in real life, but instead build upon these mythical images of them that they hold in their minds. There are porn 'stars' that have fans and followers. They win awards and are celebrated as celebrities. There are large hordes of men that are completely captivated by these women. They are lured in and snared.

Real women, and real sex, will ultimately only bring disappointment for these men. It cannot live up to their unrealistic expectations. Some men even feel that porn is simply better than having to deal with real women. They can get their orgasm on their own, watching porn, and don't feel they need sex to be fulfilled. Their porn is always ready for them, it never rejects their advances. Most of these men are fooling themselves, they have no idea what real sex entails anymore. The touch, the mutuality, the pheromones and hormones that are in play. Sex has been reduced for them to voyeurism ending with a mild self-induced orgasm. Nonetheless, this mild sensation of arousal has them hooked. Their brain loves the experience, it loves seeing naked women, and it keeps wanting to go back for more.

Masturbation by watching porn will never bring actual satisfaction. It will bring a brief temporary release of desire, but it will not have a lasting positive effect on how you are feeling. While we are talking about Narcissus, it is funny to note that there is also a positive correlation between how many hours men spend time watching porn and how narcissistic they are. The more porn men watch, the more self-absorbed they become. It individualizes, or better said atomizes the men; it places them outside of the community.

How could it get to the point where these men favor porn over real sex? Men that consume porn are even less likely to marry or engage in long-term relationships as they consider porn to be a sexual equivalent and proper substitute. Every time they watch porn, their brain releases happy hormones. Dopamine, endorphins, oxytocin, and so on. These feelings of bliss are then linked to the activity they are performing while experiencing these hormones. It is our bodies way of rewarding our good behavior. Our bodies tell us yes, it is a good thing that you are doing now, let me reward you with this happy sensation. Our body does the same when eating a hamburger. It rewards us for consuming so many calories and not letting our body starve. However, hamburgers are still real food that actually gives us a feeling of fullness and satisfaction. Although too many hamburgers are bad, it is still a real thing. Porn, on the other hand, is a synthetic super stimulant designed to confuse our brains with a never ending novelty. These reward-mechanisms are the same as our cavemen-forefathers had, and that is what they are designed for.

Your brain rewards you because it believes you are trying to procreate, and that is why it makes you feel good for a bit. We know that for porn-users, this reward system is malfunctioning. Their reward system in the brain is smaller and responds less strongly to pornographic images when compared to people that seldom, or less frequently watch porn. These porn-consumers need more, and more extreme, porn to receive the same level of reward, the same level of happiness. Their brains have become dull and are no longer impressed with regular porn. Yet, it goes beyond that. Your brain is being rewired. Porn changes what your brain finds arousing - and it's no longer real women. It's porn. And only porn.

Our desire for sex, our lust, it is a natural drive. This healthy drive has guaranteed the continued existence of our species. Frankly, any human without this drive has most likely failed to pass on their genes long ago. Only the horniest of all animals have survived the genetic race. Porn corrupts this natural instinct. Faced with a fertile woman that gives off an inviting look, men will feel aroused. They will feel enchanted by this opportunity to pass on their genes. Our reptile brain cannot distinguish between real life and a computer screen, our instinct treats both the same way. In their frustration, these men are left to their basest of desires and have no choice but to provide themselves with a helping hand. Their brain sends out an irresistible message, an order to mate with the women they are looking at. Drop whatever it is you are doing and go pass on those genes, this is how your genes have survived for so long. The brain cannot recognize this woman is thousands of miles away and it is a recording from the past. The brain does not realize that this is not a real chance of reproduction.

In the past, there would be a limited number of women in the tribe or village that men lived in. An even smaller number of these women would be eligible for seduction and mating. Now, there is an endless supply of supple female bodies spread out in front of us. Our brains love this novelty, every woman a new opportunity to breed and create new life. Since such situations were rare in the past, our brain motivates us to keep going, to go for the next orgasm soon. After all, it is our job as men to impregnate these enchanting women before our competitor gets to them, and before our opportunity with them has ended. Sometimes this novelty effect is referred to as the Coolidge effect.

Male rats will tire after a while with their mate, time to ejaculation increases and sperm count per ejaculation lowers. Yet what happens when we put a new, different, female in the cage? Time to ejaculation drops and sperm count increases. The rat orgasms quicker and with more sperm in their load. What happens when we keep adding new females into the cage? The rat will continue procreating with new females until it nears starvation. The rat's brain recognizes this once in a lifetime opportunity and takes maximum benefit. The dopamine-rush overrides all other necessities to stay alive. The rat lost control and just kept on going, making the most out of this unique opportunity. After this, the rat is so exhausted he requires time to recover from this extraordinary effort, for he is on the brink of death.

Men have this opportunity every time they connect to the internet. Our brains are not designed to encounter hundreds of new women in a single browsing session. Our deep, natural, wiring goes nuts in sending off signals to continue procreation. It doesn't know that it's all fake. The deep, reptile or tribal part of the brain, is easily fooled as it does not rely on rational thought. This part of the brain sits deeper than the more modern rational part.

Moreover, whenever such a sexual thought enters their mind, it becomes very tempting to open up a website and watch these women. It is so easy to find. We remember from the last time that we watched porn that it will feel good to watch these women. Our brain will unleash rewarding hormones and make us feel great. It becomes so very tempting to settle our sexual urge by a browsing session and some self-love. The problem is that as we observe hundreds of women, our brain wakes up and urges us to go again soon. It puts us in a hyperactive sexual state, to utilize this once in a lifetime opportunity at passing on our genes. At what point should we consider it an addiction? Is using porn once a month an addiction? Should it be weekly? Or only for those that browse such sites multiple times a day?

We might wonder at what point does it start to change us. When does it start to change how we feel and how we act. How frequent should porn use be for it to truly impact our lives? Or perhaps we should admit that to a certain extent we are all addicted, for objectively voyeurism is not very fun when there is no chance of getting involved. Does porn not affect all of us, even the ones that watch it infrequently. Has porn not shaped our entire society?

Porn is very much like an addiction. Plenty of men will have attempted to stop watching porn, only to be lured back in soon after. The anonymity makes it less shameful to indulge in this addiction as nobody else is watching you. Nonetheless, we can see that porn has the same effects on the brain as other addictive substances and triggers the same mechanisms in the reward circuits of our brain. For those that believe they are not prone to addiction, we will show throughout this book how porn affects you regardless. Your masculinity is affected by consuming porn whether you watch it compulsively as an addict, or out of your own free will as a hedonist.

For most addictive substances, we make them illegal or hard to obtain. We have institutions to help those that become addicted. Porn here is a blind spot, and it is one of the issues we will need to tackle in the 21st century. A blind spot is perhaps the wrong term, as the problem lies more with the general denial of negative consequences of porn, than of ignorance of the widespread usage of porn. Perhaps it is one of the worst types of addiction, where men constantly chase something they cannot really obtain. It certainly affects more people than any other substance. Although there are no direct physical injuries caused by porn use unless someone would masturbate until their penis is sore, there are many psychological effects. Indirectly porn can lead to mutilation of the body and self-harm, a point to which we will return in the topic on transgenderism. Furthermore, the mental consequences can become apparent in physical problems too. These effects can be as far-reaching as bringing on depression or even erectile dysfunction. Erectile dysfunction here is not caused by problems with the flow of blood, but by difficulties to feel aroused in a circumstance where porn is absent. Porn creates an unattainable desire, while simultaneously being equally appealing as having your personal harem. It is this combination of limitless desire coming from our tribal brain, combined with the impossibility of obtaining true satisfaction due to it all being a mirage. Porn is fake, it's a trick on your brain.

In the end, it is repetition that truly messes with our brain. Watch porn once in your life and of course, there will be no, or minor, consequences. Watch it a few times and there is no lasting harm. Or if it has been a few years since you've watched it frequently, your body will have recovered. But many men watch porn every week, or even every day, and have no intention to stop. To their brain, porn is connected strongly to the sensation of orgasm. It knows that the firm grip of their own hand will bring an orgasm, and orgasming will unleash the dopamines that make us feel happy. The brain starts to get aroused by sitting in front of a computer, but what about the real women around it?

There is a severe risk of desensitization, with men having to resort to more extreme forms of porn . Additionally, it even lowers men's confidence in their own body and sexual performance. Men are used to watching a hundred different girls engage in the craziest sex imaginable every time they orgasm. Can they still get truly aroused having real sex with a single girl that looks less attractive than the girls in porn that they are used to watching?

At some point erectile dysfunction sets in. For the first time in history, this problem is as common among men in their twenties as it is among men in their sixties - and that metric excludes the number of young men that never talk to anyone about their erectile issues. It is not a physical problem, it is a problem in your own mind. Your mind has been conditioned by you, to get aroused from porn and nothing but porn. Your brain can never differentiate between fake and real.

On top of that, your brain's reward system is dulled by frequent intense stimulation. Although an alternative explanation for the weakened reward system may be that such people have a higher likelihood of becoming excessive porn consumers. Either way, porn damages your reward system, or there is a subset of the population that is vulnerable to porn addiction, yet lives in a society where porn is accepted as morally neutral and safe. The problem of porn persists. More so, some people are more likely to engage in compulsive sexual behavior upon seeing sexual imagery. Despite expressing a similar amount of liking to such imagery, their brains show a higher degree of desire to act upon it. This creates more difficulty to suppress these desires and show self-control and a higher likelihood of having to masturbate when watching porn.

Many say that porn is harmless, it just makes us feel good.

Yet, it makes us feel good by the same ancient logic that eating fat food makes us feel good. Our brains are used to a life of near-starvation and few single ladies around us. When presented with the luxury we have today, our brains are tricked very easily. We all admit that eating fat food all the time is not good for us, despite it feeling good when we do it. We know that our reptile brains are wrong and that we need to listen to our more highly developed rational parts of the brain. Why don't we do the same with porn? Why don't we admit that we are fooling our reptile brain, but that we should listen to our rational brain? What man would lay on his deathbed thinking 'If only I had spent more time masturbating to internet porn'. We all know that this is not what truly makes us happy. More than likely it would make us depressed. Porn use is both cause and symptom of depression in men, and it is an inescapable trap as long as the porn addiction remains.

For those that are married or in long-term committed relationships porn can create further problems in life. Men that watch porn are more likely to have loose sexual morals and are more accepting towards promiscuity and cheating. They are also more tolerant towards infidelity. Porn consumers rate their partners, wives, and girlfriends, as less appealing and sexually satisfying after watching sexual images of other women. These men report less of a sense of bonding with their wives, and the wives feel more distanced from their men. It is logical that such bonding does not take place, as usually, sex brings about oxytocin.

Oxytocin is the hormone that makes us more generous and loving towards others, it is called the love hormone or the bonding hormone. For men that watch porn, this hormone is released while they are looking at a computer screen. Their mind is bonding to the screen instead of to their wives. It should be no surprise that porn consumption can then lead to divorce. Which it often does - men that watch porn are more likely to end up divorced. Frankly, porn demolishes the cornerstone of our society, the family. Take away the cornerstone, and the whole building will eventually collapse.

Destroy the family and society will fall. It is questionable what degree of divorces can be explained by the effects of pornography, but we must acknowledge a rise of divorces correlating to the rise of internet porn.

We can see that porn is causing a multitude of societal problems, harming all that are involved.

OLD AND YOUNG

In the previous chapter, we introduced some of the problematic results of free porn accessible to all. Here, we take the existence of porn for granted, and instead use the insights from this specific popular category of porn to observe how it translates to the rest of society. We want to have a deeper understanding of what makes certain porn categories so popular, but also a better insight into how our brains respond to it. To really tackle porn, we need to understand why our brain is so attracted to it.

Teenage girls are, and have always been, a popular category. Far from being a niche market, this is one of the bigger and earliest forms. It is estimated that one-third of porn-pages include a teen girl and the search terms 'teen porn' can reach over half a million Google hits per day. Mostly, these young teenage girls are coupled with older guys. Sometimes men that have far passed the prime of their lives, but often men that are at least a decade older. It is the pornographic version of this all too familiar stereotype of an older man with a younger woman. Apart from the gay porn scene, there is no interest in videos with teenage male actors, with one exception of the 'mature woman' scene, which we discuss later on. Although, in the videos with mature women it is mostly men in their twenties that role play and pretend to be an adolescent boy.

The girls in the category are not only young, but often also skinny and with a small build. This figure is also referred to as 'petite', the French word for small. They are to look as youthful and childlike as possible, sometimes going so far as wearing schoolgirl outfits to truly show the fantasy of these girls being mere teenagers. The limit is more of a legal one rather than a constraint based on customer demand. What we mean by this is that the porn producers cannot make the girls appear as actually being minors, as this would mean they are creating porn to attract pedophiles. There has to be some indication in the video that the girl only pretends to be going to highschool and that she really is over eighteen. This does not mean there would not be a demand for porn that featured girls pretending to be fifteen or sixteen years old.

Most men, by far, are attracted to girls in this middle to late phase of puberty. Perhaps they are less interested in the mental state of a girl this young, but male bodies respond to images of girls that are showing signs of fertility. It is not perverted or unnatural, and most men know very well they should constrain such desires. It does not mean that these men are solely attracted to girls this young, men simply value any female body that they can impregnate. When men have a preference for girls in this age range, say from fifteen to nineteen, this is called ephebophilia. However, most men will feel attraction to a sixteen-year-old that has gone through early puberty and has a more mature body. Over ninety percent of men show attraction to such girls.

Ephebophilia is rather different from pedophilia, which indicates a preference for prepubescent children. Such interest is completely perverted and finds its origin in a corrupted mind. In everyday use, pedophilia is often used to refer to any sexual interest in a minor, someone below the legally defined age of consent which often stands at eighteen. Nonetheless, the age of consent laws differ between countries and can vary from eleven years old in Nigeria to twenty-one years old in Bahrain. Some countries do not have an age of consent law, but state that sex must take place inside marriage - yet these countries also allow child marriages and have girls as young as nine years old that are married.

Hebephilia is the preference for girls in their early phase of adolescence, so right in between pedophilia and ephebophilia. These are the girls around ten to thirteen years old. That a man is sexually attracted to a fifteen-year-old does not make him an ephebophile. It only counts if the man has a preference for girls that are specifically in this age bracket. The key to remember here is that attraction to the middle to late stage adolescent girls is present among almost all men on earth. This is easily explained by the understanding that men look for women that are fertile. These young girls have become fertile and are capable of bearing a child, so logically men are attracted to them. Our genes were not passed on for millions of years by men that had moral objections to having sexual intercourse with a girl whose brain had not finished developing. Besides, by that logic the age of consent should be placed at around twentyfive. This is also why it should not be placed on the same level as pedophilia, as that is a fully unnatural desire to have. Of course, all these 'philias' are still strange, as normal men do not have preferences for these age groups. Still, there may be readers that have grandmothers that married at sixteen. Should we morally condemn such behavior? If we do, then on what grounds? The countries with the lowest ages of consent, all located in Africa, are also the countries with the highest fertility rates. Women in Niger, with an age of consent law set at thirteen years old, have on average seven children per woman.

When we observe history, this couple of a younger woman and older man may be the most normal and common. When we think of medieval kings, we often picture a mature man that takes as his bride a young girl. Many princesses became queens in their early teens. However, we should not believe that this was limited to kings that abused their power to score for themselves an innocent young girl. Nor should we immediately assume that this was a traumatic experience for such a girl. Go back into any family's ancestry and you will undoubtedly find many couples where the man is older and the woman is younger. These differences could easily be five years, ten years, or more. Women in your family tree may have gotten married or even given birth while still in their teens, without this being a shameful event at the time. Only now do we frown upon such behavior and believe that children must be postponed to later in life.

Even today, look at couples around you, look at your parents, or at your own relationships, and what do you see? Even when the age gap is not as big, it cannot be a coincidence that in most cases the man is the older part of the couple. We see this same coupling take place across cultures, across religions and whichever place on earth we look. It sheds light on this all too realistic observation between male and female relationships. Men look for fertility and youth, while women look for stability and protection.

Young women are more fertile, while older and more powerful men are better able to provide stability and protection. And most of all, such men will be financially independent, a trait valued by women. Your moral view on this may be what it is, but the law of the jungle prevails. Despite having left the woods a long time ago, this rule still holds value. This does not mean that a relationship where the woman is older than the man cannot work, but they are rarer and more fragile. When the woman is the older part of the relationship, this would rarely exceed a difference of five years. A difference greater than those five years will put immense pressure on the couple if it wishes to have children together. The woman will have passed her peak fertility and is in a rush to get pregnant, while the man is focusing on attaining financial stability and able to postpone procreation for several more years. Such biological and financial pressures can exist even when the woman is barely older than the man, or even when they are of same or similar age. Most women want children by the time they are between twenty and thirty, while most men don't obtain financial stability until they are in their early thirties. It is no surprise that couples where the woman is older, often end up childless. It is a very logical and predictable outcome.

This logical agreement of having an older man and younger woman can also put a question mark next to the idea of true, or romantic, love. These types of relationships admit a certain practicality. In fact, all relationships succumb to certain practicality. Women leave a man that has no job or financial security. Men leave a woman that is too old to have children. The woman, physically weaker, and concerned about the well-being of her offspring, is concerned about the ability of the man to protect her and the children.

The man, admittedly, desires to use the fertile womb to continue his own genetic legacy. It is not a case of one using the other, since both benefit from this trade. It is a win-win scenario. Nonetheless, if we wish to adhere to the idea of a soulmate existing for everyone, we must also acknowledge that soulmates have certain needs to make a relationship work. We see that these needs of the sexes translate directly into our tribal brain. Men and women still look for the same things in a partner as they did when we lived in small rural villages, and the same things as when we roamed the forests. Anyone that wants their relationship to work, would be wise to recognize this general rule. The Greeks believed that men and women were two parts of a union that were separated upon birth, and in life they needed to find each other once more to become whole again. This myth implies that men and women need one another, and they need one another because there are things they cannot do on their own. Things like create the next generation.

Regardless, our modern cultural norms have abnormalized such relationships. These perfectly normal relationships between older men and younger women are shamed when the difference exceeds a few years. Relationships with more than a few years of age difference are frowned upon. Men with younger women are called dirtbags, sleazy and disgusting. They are said to only look for a trophy wife. Other women will express their contempt and disgust. They are shamed by society in a way that is quite uncommon nowadays. Shaming women for their behaviors is now unacceptable, but shaming a man for dating a younger woman? That is perfectly fine. The whole society will join in shaming these men. In general, it is acceptable for shaming men for being men, it is the only group in the world that can be openly criticized and humiliated with the global media applauding it. Especially when the men are famous, magazines and TV are quick to judge these men.

Why do we not see age differences in these couples anymore? Many couples have no age difference at all, and sometimes the woman is even older than the man. In part, this is due to it being odd for an older man to even meet a younger woman. Men and women, up to their mid-twenties, live in a higher-education bubble. Most of the people they meet in this period are people around their own age. Many lasting relationships are formed during this period in life, making couples with a higher difference in age less likely.

On top of that, since people stay in education until they are at least twenty, it creates a blocker to a relationship. People believe they should think about settling down only after completing their education and having worked for a few years. This leaves a gap of only a couple of years between their first promotion and the time when their fertility begins to drop. The biggest reason may be that women are conditioned to find it creepy when they are approached by a man that is older than them and ready to start a family, they are not accustomed to this mindset and fail to comprehend how natural it is. Young women across the world are encouraged to try the party lifestyle first. They are then encouraged to make a career first. By the time they look for a serious relationship, they are not that young anymore.

Forcing girls to date within their own age-bracket creates these unnatural relationships where both are close to the same age. It is arguable that this creates a lose-lose scenario. Of course, we do not imply there should be no age of consent laws, or that we should not protect our children from dirtbags. Additionally, those in a position of power that abuse children absolutely need to be in jail. But we need to be culturally more accepting towards a thirty year old man with a twenty year old woman that both consent to this relationship. A difference of ten to twenty years is sufficient for the men to be financially stable while the women are in their peak fertility.

Perhaps it could be a factor in the insanely low fertility rates, as men and women are ready for procreation at different ages. Current relationships have created a huge mismatch, leading to the postponement of having children. By the time couples are financially ready for children, the woman may struggle more with conceiving a child at the age that she is at.

Porn here shows us what men desire; young and fertile women. A taboo in the modern world. Shame on men for pursuing their instincts. This fantasy of having a younger woman is nonetheless very alive among men. Porn gives us insight into these fantasies. The fact that such relationships have become taboo, has only made it a more tempting fantasy for these men. It has become something they can only achieve in porn. Unfortunately for many of them, porn is as close to this fantasy as they can get. It shows us that although our culture has changed regarding the acceptable age difference, our innate desires have not changed. Our tribal mind is the same as it was before. Men live in a cultural cage, where they are not allowed to pursue what they really want, for if they do they would be publicly shamed and humiliated.

The point here is not to provide a justification for men to watch porn with 'teens' in the videos, there is never a justification for watching porn. The point is also not that old men should all start dating teenagers, especially if they are not even sixteen yet. Our criticism of the age of consent applies only to those that seek to build a lasting relationship, not to those that wish to trick and abuse these girls for hedonistic casual sex - only to leave the girl behind ruined. The point here is understanding male natural tendencies, understanding what drives us and what it is that makes these videos so appealing. As Sun Tzu said in his Art of War, we must understand our enemy. With this knowledge, we create an ability to resist watching porn, as we can identify our deeper desires and recognize that porn offers no solution.

OEDIPUS AND MOMMY ISSUES

Older men may have their focus on teenage girls, for younger guys the opposite appeal is present. Mature women, mothers, MILFs (a MILF is a Mother I'd Like to Fuck, for those unfamiliar with the terminology so common in porn) and even pretended incest with their mother have become popular categories in porn. Where incest goes too far for some, there are thousands of videos involving 'stepmothers', a subtle difference. On first sight, it would appear Freud had been onto something when saying all men had an Oedipus-complex. For the truly odd ones out, the term GILF was invented as well. The G stands for Grandmother, the rest of the letters have the same meaning as before. Post-menopausal women are strangely (obviously, since men look for fertility) not as common to be featured in the adult movies, but it does happen.

Let's clarify up front that mothers can be very attractive and many women age gorgeously, looking just as great in their thirties and forties as they did when they were twenty, sometimes even better. Often, likewise, women never again attain the beauty they possessed in their youth. It is not the point of this chapter to imply that it is strange or unnatural to be attracted to such women, after all these women are still fertile and have proven their capability of birthing children, but it is the point to understand the mind of the people that search for this specific type of material. Why search specifically for a woman that is significantly older than yourself? It completely counters the natural tendency we saw in the previous chapter. Above all, if a man is truly attracted to the more mature women, it would be more suitable to find and meet one in real life, rather than being drawn to the fake version that is broadcast online. Unfortunately men that are pulled into porn lose their interest in meeting actual women and end up alone with their internet connection.

What is the Oedipus-complex, and the myth of Oedipus? Oedipus, the hero of an ancient Greek myth, is famous for having murdered his father and made love to his mother. Although for Oedipus these acts were committed out of ignorance and were accidental, Freud claims that boys actually have this desire. A desire to the full affection of their mother, for which they would need to first kill their father to be able to obtain it. With their father out of the way, the mother can devote all her love to them. Despite being widely accepted as a genius, Freud never really gave any evidence for this claim. His work was rather unscientific and fully 'unfalsifiable' to user a term created by Popper. Unfalsifiable means that there is no observation that would prove his theory to be false. Freud would explain any dreams a boy had about his mother as a desire to have sex with her, and an absence of dreams about his mother as a subconscious denial of the desire. No matter what you thought, dreamt about, or said, Freud would find a way to explain it in a way that suited him and his theory. That makes his theory unfalsifiable, as there are no circumstances or results that would prove him wrong.

You could say Freud was a fraud, when it comes to making a worthy scientific contribution. That is not to say that none of his writing were intellectually stimulating and interesting, but some of his fame may be poorly attributed. Even the name he picked for this complex, invoking the name of Oedipus, seems poorly chosen. Oedipus himself wanted nothing more but to avoid fulfilling the prophecy that he would sleep with his mother and kill his father. He did not know he had committed these acts. He only found out after his father was already dead, and his mother had already given birth to several of his children. Yes, he didn't have sex with her only once, he fathered multiple children with his mother. He was devastated when he found out that his wife was also his mother that had given him away as a baby. Hence he had never recognized his parents, he was raised by strangers that had adopted him. When he killed his father, he took him for a stranger with no connection to him. Before he bedded his mother, she told him she was childless, so she could impossibly have been his mother. Sadly, she lied about being childless. Oedipus, beyond all doubt, did not have an Oedipus-complex. He tried desperately to avoid his fate. As is common in Greek myths, destiny cannot be cheated.

We have no reason to believe that any other man does have this Freudian-Oedipus desire, and it may only have been present in Freud's twisted mind or perhaps it came into existence by his complete miscomprehension of the Greek myths. Some men may exist that have fetishized their own mothers, but this is a tiny group of perverted men, rather than a widespread occurrence. But if this is not the reason as to why this is a popular category on all adult websites, then what is?

This category of porn should not bring people to believe that these boys are fantasizing about sex with their own mother. Incest as a porn category is getting more popular, but this has more to do with porn consumers needing something more novel and extreme to feel aroused, than that they are interested in committing incest. The taboo of watching a mother and daughter in the same video is what intrigues them, not a fantasy about their own family.

Beyond that, every sane person is fully aware that the people that are acting in the video are not actually blood relatives. Broadcasting actual incest would be illegal in most places, although such videos may very well exist on the big websites as it would be impossible to check if anyone in the video is actually a blood relative to someone else. The Japanese especially have a kink for some family fun in their creations. In fairness, the Japanese are known for their odd taste in porn. Their country's preferences may offer us a glimpse into our own future. All their porn has a certain shock element. Despite that the inhabitants of the land of the rising sun create such videos, they don't appear to engage in incest in real life either. They are so consumed by porn that they barely engage in any sex at all any more.

The parts of the world where we do see incest taking place on a national level, are centered around the Middle East and South Asia. There, it appears to have its roots in tradition and religion, instead of finding its cause in individual desires. Arranged marriage brings cousins together to make sure that they keep any wealth they have in the family. Over the generations, this inbreeding leads to genetic defects and mental retardation. The European aristocracy and banking dynasties shared this tendency towards incest. They desired to keep their great fortunes within the family, if the wealth were to spread to a larger group of people they would become less powerful.

The great family of the Habsburgs followed the same routine. Their line in Spain ended in 1700 with the death of Charles II. Charles was born to a father that was also his mother's uncle, and this level of inbreeding continued up the family tree. Charles suffered various rare illnesses and was overall weak and frail, possibly caused by the inbreeding over the generations. He died childless and may have been unable to father a child, due to his genetic condition. It is no surprise that humans generally respond with disgust to the mere thought of incest, and cannot comprehend the thought process of those that commit the act. The disgust goes beyond a sense of immorality and hits upon a deeper instinct telling us that this is unhealthy. We must acknowledge the reason for the existence of this category is neither the Oedipus-complex, nor a hidden taste for incest.

What plausible explanation can we find? When we attempt to analyze this category, what does it really show us. What can we see is going on. We can see that it is more of a substitute-mother that has some motherly characteristics, but is categorically different from their own mother. For these boys, watching teenage girls in porn is perhaps too close to reality. It is too confrontational. They have no success with the girls of their age around them. Many will have been rejected by some of these girls, or insulted by others. Teenage girls are not known for being the kindest and warmest people in the world. If they would watch teenage porn, these real-life experiences would break the fantasy. We would expect to find the social outcasts that are unpopular with the girls of their own age as being more likely to search for this category.

Another reasoning is that these boys are surrounded by such girls, girls that are still growing into their adult-style bodies and are not fully developed yet. Some boys may have a sexual appetite that is more advanced for their age. Watching women that are a few years older offers something different, something new. They are already bored of the teenage girls and look for slightly more extreme or provoking porn. Different men will have different reasons, and find a different niche within this category. The outcasts will search for the warmer and kinder porn discussed below, those with a more mature taste in women will simply look for women with bigger curves than they are used to seeing.

Regardless, the socially awkward boys that get little positive attention from the girls in their age bracket may be more likely to search for mature women, than the jocks that are dating the cheerleader. For the popular jock, it is easier to insert a young girl into his fantasy, as it matches his experiences in real life. For the social outcasts it is different - but note here that in the high school setting most boys can be considered social outcasts, as it includes everyone that is not one of the most popular boys. In their minds, these young girls are linked to their sneaky classmates that gossip about them. It is not what they are looking for.

Their desires are in a way more innocent than an actual desire to procreate. They are not drawn in by the visible fertility of these mature women. They are perhaps still too young and immature for that. Watching older women creates a way out of this problematic situation that they are in with the girls around them and allows them to fill a void. A void caused by a lack of warmth and nurturing, something they are missing as they are maturing and still on the way to finding their own identity. As innocent as such reasons to view porn may be, it is the first step for such boys into a long-term addiction.

The older women will be kind, supportive and appreciative. Their role is to show warmth and compassion. These videos will often have an extensive dialogue where the mature woman is talking in a kind and motherly voice. It is soothing to the viewer. She calms them. Perhaps it is something they have missed in their youth, where they had a mother that was often working, or was lacking in kindness when she was at home. Or perhaps the men suffer from insecurities and anxiety. Anxiety to approach a girl and talk to her, so it is comforting to have a fantasy where the woman approaches them. The mature woman is deemed trustworthy, as opposed to the devious younger girls.

This is combined with their wider hips and bigger breasts, giving these women a more womanly figure. The more mature figure is more of a novelty to the young boy. They can see teenage girls around them in school or in college all day long, but watching an attractive more curvaceous woman is a change. Overall, their desires are very different from the petite teenage girl that the older guys are missing. Mature men may also search for porn of mature women, precisely because that is what they are accustomed to. For them, this is thus a more realistic search aimed at being able to insert themselves into the fantasy.

The mature woman can lead the passive boy. It is this warmth that these young boys are missing in their interaction with real girls. It is this warmth that has been sucked out of modern society. The most important thing to notice is that in this category the men never dominate the women. The men take on a passive role, while the kind-hearted mature woman does the seduction. This passive role is what makes it unnatural, as in nature men are the ones who dominate. Good sex follows the rules of nature, a dominant man and submissive woman. Immersion into the video needs to be made easy. Often this porn is shot from the point of view of the male performer. It is created in this way so that the viewer can truly pretend to be a part of it. Except for the part that instead of having a real woman kneel down in front of them, gently taking hold of their penis; it is their own hand that has a firm grip and they are obsessed with what is going on on a computer screen in front of them.

This firm grip is sometimes called the 'death grip', as it makes the penis accustomed to a grip much tighter than a vagina, or even an asshole, will ever be able to offer. On that note, some men may prefer anal as the firm grip reminds them more of the strong grip of their own hand. In every other way, beyond the firmness of the grip, the vagina feels ultimately better than the anus. Anal does, however, add some degeneracy and adds to the submission of the woman. Anyway, let's return to the boys practicing this death grip while watching the video.

As somewhat pathetic as it may be, they can pretend that this woman is actually talking to them. That the warmth she is showing, she is showing to them. Her compliments and appreciation are directed towards the camera. Again, the viewer uses this point of view (POV) porn to trick their own mind. The viewer takes on a passive role, allowing the mature woman to seduce them and to give them a handjob or a blowjob.

When sex does occur, it is often after an invitation coming from the woman. She takes the lead, she pushes for sex. The male performer pretends to be a young, insecure boy, that is not comfortable with his sexuality yet. A role that the viewer can easily connect with, for it is exactly what they are. The male performer in the video is usually a guy in his late twenties, and luckily not very good at acting. If the actor would actually be a young, insecure boy, the entire scene would likely just be cringy and kill all sexuality. For some reason bad acting has always been accepted in porn, perhaps Tom Cruise would fit right in.

Anyway, as always the focus in the video is on the woman. The woman portrays the experienced lady that introduces him to the world of sex. This is what the young viewer desires. They want someone to hold their hand as they progress into the scary adult world of penetration and sex. It is the world they fantasize about and are mesmerized by. They are scared of having sex, uncomfortable with the thought of having to impress a girl in bed. Impressing a girl in bed will only get more challenging as they are sexually inexperienced and consuming large amounts of porn; it is the magic formula to acquire early onset erectile dysfunction. The embarrassment caused by that at their age will only block their actual experience and push them further down the rabbit hole; or perhaps saying they are pulled further into the black hole would be more suitable.

Rather than facing humiliation for their ED - erectile dysfunction - in the real world, they stick to their comfortable virtual reality. They are soothed by this woman, she knows they are inexperienced and she has low expectations. Low expectations are great for those that experience sexual anxiety, which is what this is all about. They are encouraged by listening to this woman as she utters words of encouragement to the male performer, affirming what a great job he is doing. Just like a child learning how to ride a bicycle, these boys desire compliments as they are learning a new skill.

The men that view this are passive and scared. They feel uncomfortable and out of place in the world of sex. This is only exacerbated by having their primary experience with the world of sex by watching porn, creating a wholly unrealistic image and setting insane standards in their own mind. The more they watch such porn, the less suitable they become to have sex with a real woman. Most women would not want to take a young boy and be their teacher, women do not value virginity in a man. At most, a few highly religious churchgoers may say that they value virginity in a man, as it shows the man values their God and is serious about the commitment. What they won't value is his lack of sexual prowess when they reach the bedroom on their wedding night.

No woman enjoys watching a man fumble around, looking to find the right hole, and generally oblivious to what parts he is touching and how he is touching them. If you want to demolish a woman's state of arousal, then act like a virgin when having sex with her. Men have much less of a problem with having sex with a virgin girl, since women usually take the passive approach to sex there isn't much for her to do, or for her to do wrong. She likely won't provide them with a mindblowing night, nor with a topnotch blowjob performance, but the man's aroused state will be easily maintained by the mere touch of her supple body.

A man will eagerly introduce a girl into the adult world of sex, he will be flattered by being the first. He is aroused by the woman giving him a gift that she can only give to a single man in her lifetime. The gift of anal virginity is an alternative, and still somewhat flattering, but a lot less special and incomparable to that of the real virginity. That is not to say that some men may be frustrated occasionally when initiating sex with a virgin, due to the trouble of being able to insert their penis easily and the flow of blood that may follow. The first night can be messy and uncomfortable.

In short, the sex with a virgin will be very different from their porn-inspired expectations. Yet the only men truly bothered by that were the ones looking for some casual sex after a night out, nothing beyond a quick lay to release their desire. A man that has feelings for a woman will always be happily surprised to hear she is, in fact, a virgin - unless she follows that statement by saying she wants to keep her virginity and denies him the access to sex with her. That could cause frustration to take place.

This is not meant to shame women that are not virgins, nor is the point here that women that are not virgins are appreciated less.

It is only to say that a woman that is a virgin is not valued more lowly than a woman that has lost her virginity. For men, on the other hand, having the status of virginity is cause for insult and ridicule by men and women alike. It is all too common for women to insult men by calling him a virgin. Virgin men, clearly, have a lower value than their non-virgin counterparts. Women are very different from men, a woman wants a man to take charge and lead her. Something a virgin man cannot do.

For any virgin men reading this, don't take this to mean that you can improve your performance or expertise by watching porn. That is wishful thinking, and the opposite is true. It will only make you worse. Virgins that are addicted to porn are in the worst possible place, and should expect to experience ED when they first get close to a girl.

The only place where women enjoy taking the lead on a younger guy, is in these mature videos. Watching such videos, these boys only deepen these completely wrong behaviors and will face a more difficult reality when they do have real sex. If they do end up having real sex, they will likely find it uncomfortable as they will be expected to be in charge. They will have sex while longing back to the comforting virtual arms of this mature woman and the privacy and solitude of their own bedroom.

There, in their solitude, they were able to control their anxiety and insecurities. Now they are exposed and vulnerable in front of a real woman, a position for which some confidence is required. Sadly, we no longer teach our boys to be confident. In fact, we no longer teach boys how to be a man - we only warn them about the supposed dangers of masculinity. Boys growing up are lost when reaching the age that they should acquire confidence, some flock to groups of male friends that build confidence together, others simply fail to become confident. Boys are desperate to find places where they can learn about masculinity.

Global media portrays a sickening image to these young boys in the form of so many sitcoms and romantic comedies. In all these shows, it is the insecure nerd that fancies a girl, but the girl is dating some asshole, a real douchebag. In time, the girl leaves the asshole who treats her poorly and settles for the confidence-lacking nerd. She finally sees how foolish she has been and what a nice guy the nerd has always been to her. The Big Bang Theory is a prime example for this, where a hot girl constantly dates buffed up guys, until she finally falls in love with our shy and nerdy scientist-protagonist. Now, it can happen that a girl falls for a nerdy guy, that is not the problem. The problem is that the buffed up guys, the assholes, they are always portrayed as the bad guy. As evil. The opponent. The all-brawns-no-brains kind of guy. A completely wrong depiction of what manliness is about.

Rarely, are they depicted as a simple confident nice guy that happens to work out at the gym. Why would a man not be fit and not be a douchebag? Why can men in these shows not possess true virility? They pose a false dilemma, implying that men need to choose between being intelligent and staying in shape. Is it better to be a scrawny nerd, compared to a foolish brute? Who knows, but a man that possesses virility combines both. Shows like this make guys ignorant towards understanding women and their desires. So these young men watch material that gives them a fully distorted view of how women behave in relationships and in bed, skewing their expectations of reality. With such a perverted ideal image of sex and relationships, real sex can never compare as the two are fundamentally different.

The passivity finds its origin in this type of porn being firstly a desire for warmth and compassion. A way to cope with their social anxiety. Only as a secondary effect does it become sexual. The viewer really longs for intimacy and physical contact, not so much for penetration. Nonetheless, by watching the video they will become aroused and start to masturbate, but it can not fill the actual void that they have. The void is something porn can never fill, it is this human intimacy, this closeness to another, that is missing. It is smelling someone, feeling someone and tasting someone that is all missing. It is having the warmth of a woman that cares about you and shows you affection that these men lack.

A unique strength that women have, this affection, cannot be substituted by any male bonding. It can also not be substituted by anything on the internet. Today, many men lack it and they don't understand how to acquire it. And in this desperate search for affection, men stumble upon a type of porn designed just for them. Porn, however, by its nature, is unable to fill the void and leaves only greater dissatisfaction. Moreover, porn stuns their development into true men that have embraced their masculinity and are able to attract women.

INTERRACIAL, INSECURITY AND LOW SELF-ESTEEM

Porn features black men. The category called interracial is in fact merely a place to show white women having sex with black men. Despite there being many videos of white men engaging in sex with Asian or Latina women, this is not generally placed in the interracial category. Interracial is more or less a euphemism for this black on white version of porn. Black male, white female. Any race of male, black female would be found under the term ebony. Ebony refers to the darkness of the women, as ebony itself is a term for a tropical tree that provides dark timber. In porn, ebony refers to a black female. Any race of male, latina female will be found under the term latina. Any race of male, Asian female will be found under the term Asian. Despite that the race of such men will often be white or Jewish, as most men in porn are, no distinction is made in these categories. The distinction on the race of the male is only present in this interracial category, which is almost exclusively black males and white females. Latina or Asian women with black men would more likely fall under the latina and Asian categories.

For this reason, it is an exceptional category in porn. Somehow, the appeal in this type of porn is not what type of women is involved, but the type of men that are involved. It has risen from being a niche market, to being pushed into the mainstream in recent years. You cannot open up a porn website without seeing this category on the front page. Greg Lansky is single-handedly responsible for a big part of this growth by founding the website called 'Blacked' in 2014. The name of the site is clear in its purpose. It exclusively shows black men and white women; whereby the women are so-called 'getting blacked' by having sex with black men. Lansky also founded the sites Tushy and Vixen, which serve partially as a recruitment place where the women start off, before being pushed to participate in blacked videos. Many women will push the interracial scene to a later point in their career, and request more money for performing in an interracial video.

Interracial is the one type of heterosexual porn where the emphasis is on the male performer. What type of men would want to find specifically this type of videos? What is the driving force behind this category? Although there may be a preference for small, young girls, the category can also include the more mature women. The difference is purely the race of the male involved.

The men chosen are often relatively young and in good shape. Above all, even more so than already is the case for male porn performers, the black men need to possess an above average sized cock. Only the exceptional black men with the largest penis that the porn industry can find are put to work. These physical traits are a necessity for the genre. White men can become a male porn performer with an average looking body, but a black man cannot. Again here we see that a lot of emphasis is placed on how the male performer looks. His cock is at the centre of this category. What is the heterosexual appeal in that?

Some claim that interracial porn is more aesthetic. It simply looks better. There is an interesting effect on the contrast between the black and white. If this were true, then it would be similar for black women and white men, but this is not generally included in this category. Rather than it being entirely about race, it would be about a more artful genre of porn. Now Lansky does claim that porn is like art, but his focus is clearly on setting black men up with white women, more than making artsy videos that are in other ways inspiring. Surely there are other ways to produce art, if that is the supposed goal. Bringing art to porn should be possible in a variety of methods. This can be achieved in many other ways than interracial sex. What artist recreates the exact same piece of art over and over again with slight variations?

His idea that what he is doing is art and the ones having sex on camera are performance artists is only believable by those that have bought into the modernist idea that anything can be art. Yes, if Duchamp's urinal is art, then by that logic porn could be art. Your holiday pictures can be called art as well. Art is created for being beautiful to look at and inspire, porn is there to arouse and urge men to masturbate. Referring to porn as art is an insult towards Rembrandt and Van Gogh.

That it is about the contrast simply does not sound believable, and we should ignore this deceiving claim. Anyone using this pretense that it is more artistic, is merely aiming to deceive and hide their more brutal and true reasons for watching it. The appeal most certainly does not lie in the aesthetics.

A more plausible explanation is that the interracial scenes are meant to be humiliating. They portray a hatred towards women. In this logic, the black man is comparable to the savage. Untamed, animalistic, brutal and dominant. It is no surprise, following this logic, that the main theme here is the black man's large penis. The so-called 'big black cock' or BBC for short - not to be confused with the British Broadcasting Company. Note that the reason the men are cast is not merely for having a big cock, for men of any race could have a big dick. It is this special combination of both black and big. Such scenes are never romantic or designed to portray warmth. They are there to portray more dominant sex, where this brutish man takes the weak and feeble woman, whether she wants it or not.

The appeal behind such scenes is more closely resembled by beastiality, where women are made to have sex with dogs or horses. Well aware that this is a controversial claim; do not confuse this for us saying that black men are equal to these animals. Yet, the role of both the dog and the black man is to serve as a humiliating, though pleasurable, punishment for the women. The point in both is for the woman to be humiliated, but to simultaneously enjoy this sinful pleasure. It is a taboo that is fetishized.

Viewers of this type of porn have inherent racist beliefs, for such beliefs are necessary to consider it a disgrace for a woman to have sex with a black man. Since the idea behind the porn is to humiliate, and the men used are exclusively black, it is a logical conclusion to say that the men that view it find it humiliating for the woman to have sex with a black man.

"I also look at racism in pornography. Which very few people have actually ever looked at. Now, what's interesting, is [that] 1 in 4 films released into the market is called 'Interracial' and this is [involving] a black man and a white woman and this is geared to white men. So the question becomes, 'Why do white men want to watch black men penetrate white women over-and-over again?' and I was really thinking about this because it was not that long ago that black men got lynched for even the 'threat' of such a thing. So what's going on? And then it dawns on me: If indeed pornography is about the debasement of women [then] what better way in a racist society to debase a white woman than have her penetrated over-and-over again by a body that has been marked as 'demonized,' as being seen as deviant. I.e.: The black male body."

- Dr. Gail Dines

It is different for the category of 'ebony' porn, which indicates the woman in the scene is black. Often in those scenes, the man is also black. Unsurprisingly it is the most popular porn category throughout sub-Saharan Africa. Only American black men have a preference for white women. Despite that, it appears that black men prefer to see the women from their own society, rather than interracial scenes, because the ebony category is equally popular in the areas of the United States that have many black inhabitants.

In fact, strange as it is, interracial porn usually does not show up anywhere in the most used search terms of any porn site, but does show up frequently on the front page. It is a niche that appears to be stimulated by the porn industry. It does not fall under any of the top searches, but it does fall in the top of porn produced. This funding provides the access to the most popular girls and have them perform in blacked scenes.

There is a twist to this category where the woman greatly admires the black men. It is bordering on the cuckold scene which we will cover later on. The storyline here is often that the women are cheating on their white husbands or other similar tales. The black man here epitomizes something the white men have lost. He is the epitome of nature, where strength dominates. He appeals to the more animalistic, undeniable desires that hide inside us. The appeal is that there is pure animalistic lust involved, rather than affection or rationality.

Again, the core of this is inherently racist as the black man is portrayed as being the savage that is more in touch with human nature. Despite the stereotype being a positive one, it is positive in the same sense of the idea of the 'noble savage'. The noble savage is the idea that the uncivilized peoples that live in the jungle are more in tune with nature. They believe that such peoples experience more harmony, and show us an ideal of life that has been lost with the rise of civilization. In reality, these uncivilized tribes in the jungle have a far higher rate of death by violence than do the civilized peoples. The nobility of the savage disappears when the savage is placed under increased scrutiny, after which we can only draw the conclusion that the noble savage was nothing more than a myth.

The black man in this genre can be depicted as the sexual savage, a more modern play on the outdated and disproven view of the noble savage. There is more manliness in the black man, more testosterone, all these things that modern culture has defined as toxic masculinity. The woman is helpless in the presence of this virility and has no choice but to succumb. The woman is a simple creature, chasing her lust, even when it means having sex with a black man. Again it links in with the previous point made, as despite it being a black man, the woman succumbs to her lust. And lust she has - the whole storyline revolves around how the black men are better equipped to satisfy her sexual needs than her white partner can ever hope to achieve.

This is somewhat humiliating for the woman, that she cannot control herself. She is considered to willingly lower her value by engaging in sex with a black man. It is no surprise that some women in the porn industry refuse sex with a black performer, or charge higher prices for such scenes. Such reluctance or price demands can also be explained by racist attitudes among the women in porn, but it is odd to expect these women to have such conservative views and to agree to the role for a slightly higher price if they truly find black men so vile as we are made to believe.

Nonetheless, the idea of the sexual savage is a racist idea present not only in porn, but it has spilled over into the rest of society. The sexual superiority of the black men has become part of the zeitgeist, despite it being a racist concept. Racism in porn is alive and well, and interracial scenes only add to the existing racism and to the endurance of such stereotypes. On top of being insulting towards black men, it also insults the white men. If the black man is the sexual savage, then what does that make of the white men? They are soft and civilized, devoid of their sexual radiance. White men are no longer able to unleash the deep inner sexual cravings of women. They have become soft and effeminate, out of touch with their animalistic side. There is a similarity with the cuckold, as the white man has to watch while the black 'bull' has sex with the white woman. We will come back to the point about cuckolds in a later chapter.

Why do frequent porn consumers like to watch women get humiliated? Imagine the frustration that must come with being a powerless, compulsive consumer of porn. All this anger is building up inside the viewer, anger that cannot find a release. Such men masturbate to orgasm in anger, hoping it will calm them down, but it only adds to the frustration that they feel. What then, does humiliation do? The women are knocked from their pedestal. The women are out of reach from the viewer, who is frustrated never being able to reach her. So, the women are given a punishment. It is a step towards the more hardcore 'abuse' videos, or actual beastiality. Beastiality is mostly illegal and inaccessible on the mainstream porn sites, so this form of humiliation has remained, thankfully, a tiny niche.

"I'd like to show what I believe the men want to see: violence against women. I firmly believe that we serve a purpose by showing that. The most violent we can get

*is the **** in the face. Men get off behind that, because they get even with the women they can't have. We try to inundate the world with **** in the face."*
- Bill Marigold

Here it becomes clear why this genre focuses on the male performer. Having sex with a black man is a disgrace, a humiliation and a punishment to these women. The viewer can lean back and enjoy how these women are put in their place, how they defile themselves. This is the core of interracial porn, a category perhaps better renamed as blacked porn, featuring the sexual savage.

There is one additional trait of this sexual savage. This savagery, this dominance that the black men shows, this is the natural way that humans ought to have sex. Men of any race can have sex in a more brutish, animalistic way, and women will thoroughly enjoy it. The black men in these scenes are the men that are in control, not the woman. However, this 'rough' sex does not need to be constrained to involving men of just a single race. Nonetheless, it is a part of their virility that white men appear to have lost, or at least some of them. No wonder that they lose such virility, when all they do is submissively masturbate in front of their computers.

There is a secondary group of viewers of this interracial porn. Viewers of such videos are likely to be black American men, who can more easily relate to such videos where the male actor is also black - while at the same time living in a country that has enough white women for it to be relatable. Kanye West has stated in an interview on Jimmy Kimmel Live that blacked is his favorite porn. Perhaps his wife, Kim Kardashian, shares that preference, as she made her own blacked porn video before.

For them, this psychological analysis does not hold and it comes down to relatability. Unlike the Africans living in Sub-Saharan Africa, sex with white women is more relatable as they are surrounded by them. This alone explains the move away from ebony. Though, in a sense, for them, it can also play into the desire of the possibly unattainable white girl. This depends on whether the black men are able to get laid with a white girl or not. Whether we believe this to be good, bad or have a neutral view on it, sexual relationships for the most part take place between people of the same race - despite this rapidly changing in more recent years, partially due to the ideal of the sexual savage and women eager to experiment to find out for themselves if this is true. This change towards more interracialism is less visible in marriages.

Strangely, there appears to be more interracial porn than there is porn of simply a black man on a black female. This may be another reason that American blacks move towards viewing blacked videos instead of ebony, as there is more and higher quality content available. Also, because in ebony porn the men may be white, Jewish, or other races. For black men that do not have a huge penis, watching blacked porn may feed into their insecurities as the other men on screen unanimously possess a large dick.

Porn is made for Western consumers as they have the money to pay for it. For that reason alone we will see that most porn is made for, and viewed by, white men. Most viewers will be white men for the interracial category also. Having said that, since white men form a minority on the global level, this is likely to change as the rest of the world gains access to leisure time and high-speed internet connections. Plus money to spend on porn. Perhaps, it has already changed - nonetheless, we focus on the effects in European and American societies.

Yet these white men hold a certain grudge against women, even when they do not acknowledge it. They enjoy seeing women submitted and humiliated. Their innate racial bias plays a role in this. A bias they may not be aware of possessing. Or may not want to acknowledge in public, as in the current society admitting to any racial beliefs equals social suicide. We must keep in mind that preferring to watch an actor that is less relatable to yourself, and specifically searching for it, is an oddity. Something that demands an explanation that goes beyond the contrast between black and white.

The initial response to seeing porn would be to try to pretend that you are the actor, to place yourself in the scene. We will see that interracial porn is one of the steps moving away from that, into a more passive role. It is for this reason that interracial porn has very few 'POV' scenes, or point of view. Such scenes place the camera in such a way that you observe the scene through the eyes of the male actor. This way, it is easier to pretend to be a part of it, rather than a mere witness.

In interracial, this desire is overruled and the viewer takes on an utterly passive role. They are watching as the woman receives her humiliation, that she secretly thoroughly enjoys. It becomes a combination of voyeurism and masochism, and such videos link into the BDSM scene - Bondage, Domination, Sadism and Masochism. You may have noticed that as we try to point out that porn makes men passive voyeurists, we highlight specific categories that amplify these behaviors. Blacked porn is only one step removed from outright cuckoldry.

The sexual savage is a tool to satisfy the woman. The focus of such scenes thus lays on watching how the women receive this satisfaction. How this brutish animal provides her with what her reptile brain is craving so much. It is about total submission and female ecstasy. The pleasure of the men is here less relevant, as the viewer is not relating to him. As one person describes it on an online forum:

''I can't stop imagining myself as the girl when I'm watching straight porn. Why am I like this? Why can't I just be regular guy who wants to f*ck the girl not be the girl?''

Of course your brain connects to the protagonist receiving the pleasure. The pleasure of the black man is only brought into focus when it is about the woman submitting to him, giving all of herself to pleasure him. In essence, in interracial scenes more than in any other category, the male actor is reduced to being there for their appendix. The sexual savage is there in the function of a tool.

This observation goes beyond interracial porn though. Everywhere in porn the man is there mostly for the sake of swinging his dick around to either humiliate or sexually satisfy the girl. Whatever the man is experiencing, what sensations, are irrelevant. No man enjoys watching another man's face as he reaches orgasm. It is natural that the focus is on the woman, but what does it do with your brain when you spend so much time watching women? Does your brain not start to mirror the feelings of the main character you are watching? What does it do to your brain when you constantly watch a woman that is submissive, or even being humiliated, yet she enjoys it and you are enjoying watching her?

The orgasm of the man is connected to the smiling face of a woman, eagerly receiving the spunk on her face. At some point, you will start to connect submissive behavior, even being humiliated, with feeling joy. Urges to engage in such behavior may spring into existence, where previously there were no such desires.

There are entire internet fora that focus on the fantasy of turning into a girl. Men fantasize about having a pill that turns them into a woman for a day, or a week, so that they can experience sex from their perspective. There are so-called sissy hypno videos, that purposefully aim to convince men that they want to be a submissive girl that hands out blowjobs and gets cummed on. Transgenderism and fetishization of their own body is a small step removed from that. These men no longer want to be men, they fantasize about the sexual pleasure the girls that they watch in porn are experiencing.

The obsession with the large penis, the big black cock, can definitely drive insecurity. For black men, this meme has created a belief that merely for being black they should necessarily have a large dick. For the black men that are on the lower end of the dick-size bell curve, this will create endless disappointments in the eyes of the girls they hook up with. For them, there will be no compassion or understanding. The only solution for these men is to go on a sexual retreat and become involuntarily celibate. Especially since many of these girls will be hooking up with the black men to find their own rewarding experience with the sexual savage.

Porn has made both men and women to expect every black man to be walking around with a dong the size of a cucumber, a tough expectation to beat. Superficial as it is, girls will want sex with a black man solely to experience his oversized instrument, it is both sexist and racist in one go. It is thus a harmful stereotype for some black men, but it extends to the entire black community if this 'BBC' meme is considered to be the only really positive thing about being black. The BBC meme itself is doubtful to be true. Most research that does not rely on self-reported measurement for penis size do not show large deviations between population groups. In porn, as well as in the subset of black men that have frequent casual sex, there is a strong selection bias for men with large penises that makes it an untrustworthy portrayal of reality.

The value of their group becomes limited to a single aspect, and they are in fact sexually objectified. They are reduced to only being suitable for animalistic sex, and although this is something many women desire, it is hardly a flattering picture for all black men when that is all they are respected for. Their other virtues are thereby ignored, and the black men that do not carry around a cucumber-sized piece are left with nothing at all. Moreover, black men feel that this is the only expectation that they need to live up to. They believe they are destined to be sexual, and no more.

For the white men that watch these videos, but porn in general also since the dicks will always be of the larger size, this can also create a feeling of inadequacy. They may become convinced that they are unworthy of these girls, or that they are incompetent of providing such pleasure to these women, due to their own size. In porn, the only value of a man is their dick, and some men translate this into real life. More specifically the size of their dick.

Although a larger penis may bring more pleasure for a woman, it is not the only worth a man has. Most penises are within a narrow range when it comes to size, with the very rare exception of the micropenis. Yes, if you have a micropenis that is less than a few centimeters long, then you do have a serious problem. It would be difficult to penetrate, let alone stimulate, a woman. Fortunately, this condition is extremely rare and does not apply to the average guy getting indoctrinated by porn. So otherwise, you'll probably be fine with the size that you have.

Of course, it is nice for a man to have an above average sized penis, there is no denying that. However, men should not let it ruin their self-esteem if they are comparing themselves to porn actors. Nor is it the man's primary purpose in life to bring sexual pleasure to a woman. Moreover, a huge penis is not a requirement to bring sexual pleasure to a woman. Despite being helpful in achieving that goal. Various women prefer various sizes, as the depth of their vaginal canal also differs. You could indeed be too big, when you are thrusting against her cervix and causing too much pain. When this is the case, it will probably not be too difficult to find a different woman that is more appreciative of your condition.

Furthermore, if you are a fan of anal sex you should probably rejoice in not being too big, as it will be a barrier for women to let you enter them in that way. How you stimulate a woman sexually is not what defines you as a man. Although, any sane man would attempt to master that skill. It will keep your wife happy and satisfied. That topic we will not cover in this book, but you may search for material elsewhere. Perhaps this book will provide you with some clues and insights as to how the female psyche works, which may be beneficial to you in those endeavors. Frankly, many men struggle severely to understand women and what they desire in bed. The women are desperate to find what their natural state demands, and end up frustrated when no man is able to supply it. In order to provide it, men need to rediscover their virility. Or else, men may end up fantasizing about black men that possess such sexual prowess and still know how to have sex. Either men must embrace their instinctual way of having sex like an animal, or wither away into cuckoldry.

The point here is that men that watch such videos are often the same men that feel somehow inadequate themselves. This lowered position that they give themselves is compensated by also lowering the status of the women they watch. And their status is lowered by having to engage in sex with black men, our sexual savage. The women must be humiliated, to be brought within reach of the viewer. The viewer can no longer enjoy watching these women that he has idolized, without attention moving towards his own insecurities. These are not confident, self-assured men.

The genre is ultimately based on inherent racist beliefs, as those that do not find it humiliating for women to have sex with black men, will not go searching for this specific category. Unless, he has so lost touch with his sexual roots, that he stands by in amazement to see a sexually confident man engage in sex with a woman. Though, those men could look for any kind of dominating porn instead of specific interracial porn. We can formulate a general rule for insecure men that view porn. The more porn a man watches, the more insecure he becomes. The more insecure the man feels, the more humiliating porn he will search for. The more porn he consumes, the more insecure he becomes, and so on, ad infinitum. You cannot raise your own level of confidence by watching someone else get humiliated. The only way to become more confident as a man, is to reject porn all together.

THE MORE THE MERRIER

Orgies, gang bangs, whichever you want to call them. The videos are popular among both men and women, for various reasons. We can split it into two main categories, those with multiple men and multiple women, and those with multiple men and a single woman. When there are a single man and multiple women, it is generally one man and two women as part of a threeway. The psychological effect of that is generally more innocent, as it should be considered a mixture between the regular man on woman porn mixed with some lesbian aspects into the same video. Not to say there is no psychological impact, as all porn has a strong influence on your brain. Such videos are often more tender, while the focus in group sex is on a rough, dominating aspect mixed with humiliation. Chuck Pahalniuk wrote a book on the sort of group sex where a woman was to have sex with hundreds of men. The book may be in the format of a novel, but it still provides a disturbing view of the behind the scenes of such a project.

The title of this chapter is a reference to an activity in the book Brave New World, by Aldous Huxley. In this dystopian future, or perhaps in some views it would be a utopian future, the men and women have mandatory orgies to release their sexual energy. In a communist style, committed relationships were forbidden and everyone was to engage in sex with everyone else. Some people already attempt to make this world a reality, although it appears to ignore the normal human tendency to fall in love and desire exclusiveness with their partner. Many say that between 1984, by George Orwell, and Brave New World, by Aldous Huxley - it is Huxley's work that is a closer representation of today's dystopian world. Mankind has been subdued by pleasure and endless distraction, making them utterly incompetent towards any revolutionary goal. Orgy porgy may not one of his prophecies that has come true, but having everyone masturbate on their own towards a virtual world is even more successful in reaching the goal that orgy porgy was designed for - utter submission and a passive population.

Let's dive into this porn category. We will start from the male point of view. Group sex where multiple men and multiple women have sex one on one is more or less simply a multiplication of the vanilla-style pornography. The desire for this multiplication implies the viewer has a somewhat sedated response to porn due to overuse. A single video with a single woman can no longer stimulate them enough to reach satisfaction, so they are now watching multiple videos at the same time, or a video with multiple women. All of this is to keep their interest, comparable to a drug user that needs bigger and bigger dosages to reach the same high. Watching a single woman no longer gives them enough of a novelty. They constantly need to see new and different women to keep their interest going. Their brain has become accustomed to seeing dozens of naked women available in front of it. Now, when the brain sees only a single naked woman, it remains sedated. Rather than swapping between different browser pages, the man decides to watch a video that has this multitude of women.

When there are multiple men in a video, or multiple couples having sex, then who do you as a viewer relate to? The first logical answer in most cases is nobody. You are, again, an observer at a party. You are there to watch others have fun together, enjoy each other's bodies. You are a voyeur enjoying voyeurism. While at the same time, you are alone, standing there, watching, without anyone touching you. You take on a passive role compared to a whole group of people doing the real thing. You have taken on the role of outsider, far removed from the group. You are again mentally reduced to being a voyeur. Your brain has linked watching other people have sex to arousal and orgasm, rather than linking a woman touching you to arousal and orgasm.

If you become too used to this voyeurism, next time a woman will try to give you a blowjob, you will be suffering from erectile dysfunction. You are uncomfortable being a part of the scene, instead of a passive witness. You will desperately try to imagine a porn video you saw and relive those memories, while her lips move across your shaft. Sadly, as you require constant novelty, reliving the same porn movie does not work for you anymore. Real sex tends to involve only you and one woman, how healthy do you think it is for your brain to require the images of dozens of women to be able to orgasm? Do you believe it is normal that seeing a single girl naked is not enough, that it is not enough to arouse you sufficiently? No, it is a sign of a sickness - where the sickness is the addiction to porn.

Our tribal ancestors living in nature would also have such outsiders. The weaker males would stand idly by as the more dominant men would mate with the females. These weaker males would be waiting their turn for any leftovers, women that were free game once the alpha males were finished. These weaker males knew that they would be chased off by the higher status males if they came too close while they were still copulating. Some apes that are closely related to us still have such mating styles.

These beta-males were aware of their status in the group, and that they had no, or little, chance of mating. Nonetheless, they will attempt to mate once the alpha males retreat after getting tired from all the sex. Then, if they manage to have sex too, their sperm can compete.

Sperm competition is ingrained in human males and causes their loads to increase in size when infidelity is suspected, or known to have taken place (cuckolds use this to justify their fetish). A similar stance must be assigned to the porn viewer that is watching a whole group engaged in sex. Your brain recognizes your position as that of an inferior, low-status male. Your best bet for survival in the tribe at that moment is to be submissive towards the higher-status males, so that they allow you to stay a part of the tribe.

Despite not being able to mate, you should make yourself useful to ensure your acceptance into the tribe and thereby survival. Perhaps one day in the future you may have a chance to actually mate, perhaps not. Roles are not fixed and in time a beta male could become an alpha. Being a voyeur is a clear sign of being a beta. Your body language will start to portray this weak and submissive state, as your body language, subconsciously, mimics the state of your mind. Your brain recognizes you are not manly enough to take on your rightful place in society.

Your brain mirrors what you watch and do. This is how our tribal brain, our reptile brain, responds to such stimuli. Your brain recognizes the situation you're in, and will release hormones that match your role. Your neurons mirror what you are seeing. Likewise, research has shown that if you take up a lot of space, then this will make you feel more confident. This is because taking up a lot of space is a dominant trait, and you can fool your brain into believing you are the dominant person in your tribe. Your brain will accept your body posture as being the truth, and release hormones to make you feel more confident to match this. Some public speakers will raise their arms in the air before going on stage in a celebratory pose, merely to feel more confident before having to speak to hundreds of people.

We know that this is true, so would it not be logical that watching porn has a similar, though opposite, effect on our minds? Do you believe watching porn will make you feel confident? That watching another man have sex with a woman will somehow be healthy on your brain? Or, may it be possible, the porn will increase the anxiety you experience around others, as your brain recognizes your low status?

Now, next, we have the category where there are a single

woman and many men around her. An example that is popular is the 'Bukake' version where a woman receives the cumshots of dozens of men onto her body and face, covering herself in their sperm. The woman takes on a fully passive role, at most giving a blowjob or a handjob, while the men for the most part simply jerk themselves off. They are there solely to add more semen.

Clearly, this one is not about the woman having pleasure in this act. It is about humiliation and promiscuity. After all, she allows all of these men to cum on her face. She does not distinguish between attractive and ugly, or young or old. Here lies the appeal to this category, this total lack of differentiation.

For the weaker males in the tribe, such a lack of differentiation was there best opportunity to procreate. Their sperm could fight it out along the sperm of all the other men racing towards the womb. Of course, this type of video is also strongly about humiliation and degradation. Still, there are young men that idolize such videos and dream about taking part in it. They will dream of any odd chance to share their manly juices with a woman. It will surprise nobody that it is easy enough to find men willing to participate in these videos, no monetary reward needs to be provided.

To some, this idea of mandatory orgy porgy will sound appealing. They would never again have to worry about getting laid. Most men would not oppose the idea of having sex with multiple women. The idea that all these women will also have sex with every other man, is easily ignored during the fantasy.

We know that our ancestors were not as monogamous as we are now, or at least have been for the past centuries when Christianity emphasized purity. Christianity enforced a degree of monogamy, despite many people frequently breaking such rules and having multiple sex partners during their lives. Modern society has replaced lifelong monogamy with serial monogamy for the most part, combined with one-night-stands and brief flings. Serial monogamy, being monogamous at any time but moving from partner to partner over time, appears to be the generally accepted way to live.

How does monogamy look throughout history? Monogamy does not really seem to arise until we became a materialistic society and inheritance became an issue. This happened when humans ceased to be nomads, and settled down as agrarians. Nomads are not able to carry a lot of possessions around, but this problem was solved when we built houses in which we could store our wealth. Moreover, the land that someone owned now became a big part of their wealth. As this wealth and land would be passed on to the next generation, suddenly it became relevant to know who your children were.

Monogamy was a necessity for this, as there was otherwise no way of finding out whose sperm had fathered the child, if both had had sex with the same woman in a brief period of time around the conception date. DNA testing for paternity was not invented yet.

We do assume here that monogamy was not the standard in nomadic peoples, which frankly we don't know for sure. The nomads did not invent writing and we don't know much about their societal structure. It may be the case that they were already monogamous and that children were raised by their biological father. Knowing who the father was was still relevant to prevent inbreeding, but it would also provide additional support in raising the children. If they did practice monogamy, it is likely that their version of monogamy was less strict than the agrarian version. Serial monogamy would have been difficult to sustain in these tribes that often only counted several dozen to several hundred people, but also not impossible. Serial monogamy is unlikely in these relatively small tribes as there is a small group of fertile women to pick from, our current interchangeability of relationship partners is due to the massive group of potential partners to choose from.

Unfortunately, as we said, we don't know for sure how our relationships and mating behaviors looked before we started to write things down. Our oldest books are mostly religious, and these do seem to spend a lot of effort on outlining how men and women should behave. The religions came into existence after people settled down and became farmers, as large groups of people needed common rules to live by without society descending into endless blood feuds and other random killings. For as much that these religions focus on violence, they also focus heavily on relationships between men and women. Perhaps this was necessary because it was so different from the past.

It is highly questionable to what extent men and women were ever truly monogamous, but that is not to say that people were always extremely promiscuous - despite people today offering that as an excuse for their extremely promiscuous behavior. Throughout the world, people appear to settle for some degree of monogamy, and when they deviate it is out of necessity. Societies with few men, because most died in battle or other acts of violence, ended up allowing men to take multiple wives. This happened, for example, also in Islam. The wives of fallen soldiers could hereby easily marry another man, even when the man already had a wife. Societies with few women, resulted in men sharing a wife. This is very uncommon, but happened in places in Central Asia. No known society is truly polyamorous.

Perhaps we should assume that this happened partially due to biological reasons. Humans may have adhered to some form of sequential monogamy, where a man and woman would stay together long enough to give birth to a child and protect it through its infancy, but could break up and find different partners afterwards. Or simply continue together and create another child, there is no reason for them not to. The strict version of monogamy as we know it, likely started with the dawn of agriculture. This is the version that has been passed on through the ages in the form of religious writing. That is also the version that the modern world likes to push away from, ignoring the hidden benefits that it has and how natural it comes to us.

There is also some biological evidence that points in a different direction. Before, many men would mate with the same woman, akin to how bonobos still live today. DNA evidence shows that throughout history far fewer men have been able to reproduce than women, meaning that some men succeeded in having children with multiple women, while other men remained childless until death. Research has shown that men are aroused by seeing other erect penises, not due to being gay, but because of a drive to compete.

This is why porn, in general, is so effective, despite looking at another man's dick. Our penises are designed to be able to scoop out sperm when we pull back out of the vagina. The cock has an edge around, and this edge is designed to catch the seed of another man that has mated with the woman before you. This is why your cock goes limp as soon as you have blown your load. Every man goes soft after ejaculation. Staying erect would ruin your chances of procreation, as you would end up scooping out your own sperm.

A wider, thicker, penis would be more efficient at scooping out the sperm, as it applies more pressure against the vaginal walls. This would be an evolutionary benefit of a thicker penis. Moreover, a longer penis would reach closer to the cervix, and could thereby deposit the sperm closer to the egg. This would gain his sperm valuable time in competition to the others. The fact that human penises are relatively large for our body size (compared to other animal species, for example gorillas), may be an indicator towards these behaviors where multiple men deposit their sperm inside the same woman around the same time. It is only in those circumstances that these differences in size really matter from an evolutionary perspective. Since gorillas protect their harem and don't allow other males to mate with their women, they do not need a large penis.

This may all sound rather disgusting to you, to scoop out another man's seed with your own cock, but it is effective enough to ensure that you won the genetic race and are alive today. So part of the reason men love porn is that it drives the innate desire for competition. Men are turned on by seeing other men have sex, this is a fact, because it gets them ready to go next. Sadly for our porn consumers, they never get to go next. They are getting themselves ready, all worked up, for a fantasy. Our bodies are not designed to experience that on a daily basis, it eats up the energy. Worse is to fetishize it and become a cuckold.

Some of our ape-relatives still procreate this way, though over time humans become more possessive and reluctant to share. Anyone that has been in a relationship will be able to recognize that. That is not to say that we should become more promiscuous, but merely to show that this old, ancient, reflex is still present in our brains. Our brains are fooled as we are watching the computer screen, as the woman we watch is not actually in our vicinity. We cannot actually go in and scoop out the other man's sperm and try to impregnate the woman ourselves instead.

Though, as always, our reptile brain, our ape-brain, does not care about reality. It only cares about deeply ingrained reflexes over which we have little control. These reflexes are easily fooled, but this is why we have a cognitive ability to override these reflexes. It can be difficult, but in most cases we know that it is what we must do. Porn has been ignored for so long as it has been playing with our unhealthy reflexes that viewers are simply not aware that they should override them. Porn is difficult to cope with, precisely because it abuses these healthy natural instincts.

Promiscuity is simply a fancier term for slutty, they are women that allow many men to have sex with them. Nonetheless the term sounds less vulgar, which enabled Nelly Furtado to get away with having a song titled 'Promiscuous Girl'. These scenes with large groups of men, are thus to arouse this possibility of sex for the weaker men. A woman that allows the entire tribe to mate with them, may be their best shot. It may be their only shot.

The higher status male that always has access to the female womb may be disgusted by such promiscuity, but for the lower status men, such promiscuity is their shot at procreating. It is, of course, the ideal mating strategy to be the only male able to impregnate a woman, instead of having to combat the sperm of other men. Sperm competition only becomes relevant when the first option is unavailable to you. So it becomes relevant for the weaker men.

No other woman would let them have sex with them. No other woman would want to have sex exclusively with them. However, letting this weaker sperm compete with the other men for the womb? This is not as big of a deal for the woman. Especially if the woman herself is also of lower value to the tribe, and cannot obtain true commitment from the more desirable males. It is no surprise that men that consume more porn are more likely to approve of female promiscuity and more tolerant towards their infidelity - these are all ancient beliefs for weaker men.

How can women protect their offspring? If she would only mate with the strongest male, but he does not offer protection to her infant, then she cannot protect the young child. When many men deposit their sperm in her, none of those men are likely to attack her infant as it could be their own child. Chances are small that the weak male will actually be the winner of the sperm race, but the weaker male will not know this. Allowing multiple males to try to impregnate the female, ensures that none of these will harm the female or her child. French women can still apply this same strategy, as paternity testing without the mother's consent is forbidden in France and punishable by a large fine and jail time.

This is the solid logic behind this behavior. If the male knows they did not mate with a certain female, then they know the child she has is definitely not theirs. At least this logic was solid back in the violent tribal days. They could kill the child and try to impregnate her instead. Lions still do this. They will kill the cubs that were fathered by another male lion, and as the lioness becomes fertile again they will impregnate her with their own seed. Some apes do the same thing, and throw the infant against a rock to crush his skull. This has been observed in human tribes as well. The term for it is infanticide, and is basically the same as post-natal abortion. For societies without advanced medical institutions, pre-natal abortion, in other words abortion as we understand it, with the child still inside the womb, may not be possible without the right medical instruments. Infanticide then offers a solution. We can see morality is flexible and bends to pragmatism.

If this killer lion would also have had mated with the lioness before she gave birth, he couldn't be sure that these cubs weren't actually his. Due to this doubt, this uncertainty, he would likely abstain from killing them. Some animals may be able to scent if a child is actually from his blood, but people are notoriously bad at smell. An article in The Guardian shared that more than one out of every twenty-five fathers had a child that wasn't his, despite being convinced it was his own child. One telling story was a man that had been with his wife for over ten years, and had three children with her, or so he thought. When she was pregnant of the fourth child, she admitted she had cheated on him. As he requested a paternity test on child number four, he decided it may be worth it to test the other three children as well. It turned out that none of the children were his.

Clearly, sperm competition still plays a role in human procreation, although assumably much less than in the past. Most women make sure that the children they give birth to actually belong to their husbands. Still, it does take place all over the world. This is why some females let multiple males mate with them. It will guarantee none of them try to kill your child later on, and they will be more likely to offer some protection and resources when needed.

Nowadays, there is no biological necessity for such behaviors. Men are not as violent as in the past, and in any case, we have the police to keep everything under control. Nonetheless, females that are desperate to obtain protection, uncertain of their place in the tribe, may be the most likely to engage in such behaviors. Physically women will always be the weaker gender (we use gender and sex as synonyms). Evolutionary this has led women to try harder to fit into the wider group, as they would likely not survive as an outcast. Again, remember a lot of behaviors are still driven by these tribal instincts. We are not as purely rational as we like to believe. Unexplainable behaviors may be explained due to this evolutionary psychology.

Men are more likely to dissent from the group's beliefs as they could still survive on their own in the wilderness. This willingness to dissent also becomes apparent in politics and more extreme political beliefs. Women are more likely to embrace such beliefs once they are socially acceptable. We could wonder if this offers an explanation as to why women that grow up without a father-figure have the stereotype of ending up as more promiscuous.

In the ancient tribal community, not having a father figure would put you in a very uncertain position, as there is no strong male to guard you against malicious others. For such females, it would be logical to start mating with other males on a young age, and with multiple of them. Mating with a single male for protection may not be sufficient, as the male may offer some protection, but this may be not enough.

Then again it may also be due to abandonment anxiety and the belief that no men in her life would ever stick around, so as a defensive mechanism they preempt the men leaving by never getting attached to them in the first place. These women may fear that if they try to bond with a single male, that this male could desert her and leave her on her own, as her father had done before. Abandonment issues may play a big role in trying to secure a place in the tribe, without having to fear that the one man you rely on for protection will desert you. Mating with multiple males in the tribe will provide a greater cushion and provide more stability for her place within the tribe.

Do not underestimate how poorly evolved our brains are for the modern age. Although it is easy to reject such a hypothesis as mere myth, the reality is that we know little about what drives our behaviors. We do know that humans lived for hundreds of thousands of years in small tribal communities that lived as nomads in the wilderness, before settling down in agricultural societies.

The last thousands of years are hardly enough for our brains to evolve into a different set of wiring. We walked the Serengeti for hundreds of thousands of years and our reptile brain is millions of years old. We left Africa tens of thousands of years before coming up with agriculture. The few thousand years of civilization has altered our brains, but not by a sufficient amount to be well adapted for our current environment. Undoubtedly many modern behaviors can be explained when we look at how this behavior could have been beneficial for humans to engage in thousands of years ago when we lived in small tribes.

The brains that we were using back then are largely the same brains that we use now. And especially for natural acts like sex, we do use our more ancient brains for this decision making. Our more modern parts of the brain that allow us to consider the pros and cons and make fully rational decisions, hardly come into play when it is about sex.

Let's return to our weaker males. The males that normally have no option to mate and procreate. Therefore it becomes appealing to have a woman spread out in front of you that does not refuse any man. It means she will not refuse you either. This inability to refuse is also a form of humiliation towards the woman. Although in reality, the viewer is powerless and frustrated, they can now share that same lack of power with the woman that they are watching. The woman can not refuse. She holds no power any more.

The viewer can fantasize about being one of the men that is able to have sex with this submissive woman, but some viewers will start to relate more to the woman. After all, such scenes are not taken from a point of view of the male performer, but focus on what the woman is experiencing. The woman is highly desired in the video, as all these men want to get with her. A woman inside a tribe that is desired by all these men undoubtedly has access to the best genes of the alpha male, well done to her - it serves a benefit for procreation.

The viewer is likely not desired at all, so this feeling of being wanted becomes enchanting to them. They may start to fantasize about being desired, even subconsciously. This is a common principle in pornography, for multiple genres, as the emphasis is always on the woman. The woman is passive, submissive, and desired, and some men start to relate to this. They will start to desire to be the woman. As they are watching someone receive load after load of sperm onto their face, it is likely that their brain starts to imagine this is happening to them.

Now the viewer is aroused, approaching orgasm, and thinking of how it would feel to receive dozens of warm cumshots on their face. In their brain, a connection is made between receiving a facial and being in a state of arousal. So much for becoming a masculine and virile man, when our boys are fantasizing about having a passive effeminate role. Porn does not stimulate masculinity; no, porn blocks masculinity and prevents boys from maturing into real men.

SUBMISSION AND DOMINATION

Women choose to submit and enjoy it. Women voluntarily take on the more passive and submissive role in sex. She chooses to submit to the men, and she chooses to let them have their way, but it is always her choice. She could decide not to let the men have their way, and merely tease them. Despite her voluntary submission, she is still in control of the act itself. At least, in normal, real sex. That is, excluding porn where the woman is usually not in control but pressured by the men on the set. Here we focus on real sex. There the men can merely decide on the details, on the precise movements of how they will please and satisfy her. The men's lust drives them to satisfy her desires, and bring her to orgasm.

The joy and satisfaction of the men become relevant only after the woman has been pleased, she will make the man finish only after she has finished. During the act, the men take away the decision making from the woman, for decisions such as which sexual position to be in. This is again a voluntary submission from the woman, who can cease to worry about such minor details and instead surrender herself to the ecstasy of the act itself. She enjoys being taken, shutting down her thinking to focus solely on sensation. Not having to think, she can focus all the more on the pure pleasure it provides her.

The male performers, on the other hand, must focus on postponing their own orgasm and thinking of how to best please the female. Unless they simply orgasm after a few minutes and leave the woman unsatisfied, this is also an option for men. In a way this begs the question of who truly is the submissive one, perhaps we should conclude that both the man and the woman have their roles. To avoid confusion we will continue to refer to the one that takes on the passive role during the sex act as being the submissive one. Yet, both parties submit to each other's desires.

It would be wrong to think that women hereby take on a lesser role, or that they are subservient. Their pleasure is very well taken care of. Both love to please the other, the woman by surrender, the man by focus and control. For the woman having multiple men fawn over her and be willing to please her is thus a fantasy that gives her more power. More men are under her spell. Even when it is only one man, the woman takes great pleasure in feeling desired. She wants him to be rough, because it signals to her that he is passionate about her.

Sex involves a submissive and a dominant partner, but these two are equals. It must never be said that one is lesser to the other. However, both are linked to only one of the genders. Men are naturally dominant, while women are naturally submissive. Only perversions of nature swap these around. Both genders, when healthy and mentally stable, prefer to take part in their natural role allocated to them by nature. There may be exceptions where occasionally they enjoy swapping roles, briefly, but this is a little play act that should not be taken serious by either party. In those cases, the man is granting her a little wild experience by allowing her to do what she is wanting to do. This entire activity it should be clear that the man can overpower her whenever he wants to.

This dominant-submissive theme also returns in the rape fantasies that women have. Men sometimes struggle to understand how women can fantasize about rape, as it is surely a horrendous experience to go through in reality. Depending on the study one-third to two-thirds of women admit to having had sexual rape fantasies. Most women prefer to describe these fantasies as 'forced' sex over 'rape'. In legal terms there is little distinction, but their preference for the term 'forced' indicates that they don't consider the men in these fantasies as breaking the law and it silently admits that the women are happy that the man is forcing them into the sex. The studies found the greatest explanation for these fantasies was the feeling of being desired. Phrased differently, they were so attractive they were able to drive the guy crazy enough to force himself upon them.

What men must understand is that a rape fantasy always involves a man that the woman secretly wants to have sex with. They are handsome and successful, not the creepy, ugly men that are the rapists in the real world. Imagine the scenario of fifty shades of grey, where a rich, handsome billionaire takes care of a plain Jane type of girl. Failure to understand this causes some misogynistic men to believe rape isn't as bad as some women make it out to be. As if it is not traumatic to be taken by a stranger by force, not having a choice but to receive his vile sperm inside of you. This sense of being absolutely powerless can trigger anxieties and mental health issues. Real rapists should be in jail, and those that commit violent rapes, or gang rapes, should be in jail for life. Gang rapes are the biggest red flag for the emergence of a rape culture. A rape fantasy is in fact only rape by modern standards, as the woman wants to have sex with the man, but the man does not care to stop and ask her about this. Technically, she is not able to provide her consent - but only because the man does not bother to ask her.

Rape fantasies are popular, not because women are having sex with men that they do not want to have sex with, but because the men in the fantasy lose their self control. The men break their invisible chains for the sole purpose of making love to this woman. They desire the woman so much, that they have no choice but to skip the regular elements of courtship. Women put a lot of effort into how they look. The nicest clothes, hours of makeup, they appreciate men noticing this and finding them attractive. A handsome man going crazy about them is a great compliment. The keyword in that sentence is handsome. Women, during sex and in life, always seek to be desired. Knowing that they are desired, and that it is a strong desire, make them feel safe and secure. Men, take note, if you want to be good in bed you have to put in the effort to make her feel your desire.

The men must be animals. Their lust so great that they go wild, and turn into a beast. The woman enjoys being so desirable to this man that she can have this strong effect on him. She loves that her decision making element is taken away. The man simply takes her, no questions asked. She does not need to give permission. Though of course in her fantasy she does consent in her mind, she does not need to say this out loud. She may even enjoy being defenseless and having no choice but to submit to his desires. Many women are not comfortable taking conscious decisions. Take for example the scenario where a man asks his girlfriend where she would like to go for dinner. The answer, in every joke, but based on reality will be a relentless "I don't know". Women are often more comfortable in letting someone else take such decisions. When a woman ends up in bed with a guy, she is likely to describe it as "it just happened". Of course, it did not just happen. Likely, the guy put conscious effort into getting her into his bed - he made a clear decision and convinced the girl to go along with it. For the girl, it was comfortable, because she could simply go along with it as the man was leading the way.

It is telling that this is one of the most popular sexual fantasies among women. Again and again, we must conclude that for women the natural role to take during sex is the submissive role, and that women take great pleasure in this role. There may be exceptions, but many men will have experience with how a feminist girl will turn completely submissive once they take her to bed. This does not mean that these women prefer to be submissive in all aspects of life, especially at work. We are talking exclusively about the natural role during sex, and how to make it most pleasurable for both.

What women say they want in daily life, versus what they truly desire in bed, are radically different from one another. Then again, if you ever watched the comedy featuring Mel Gibson called "What Women Want" you would have already known this. We might ask ourselves if a movie like that could still be produced today, or if it would now be deemed politically incorrect for somehow pushing dangerous stereotypes. Strange that we even need to consider that, since the movie was released in the year 2000, a mere eighteen years ago.

Any man that seeks to understand women, but also that seeks to understand how to please women, must remember what women really want. Sadly, as male on male bonding has declined over the years, many men are left to figure this out for themselves. Men are lacking in male support groups in which they can talk about their life and share experiences and knowledge. It is no surprise that there has been such a rise in male-dominated internet fora where males discuss these types of topics. Alternatively, you will simply have to discover it on your own during your lifetime, by your interactions with women.

Porn upsets this natural dynamic for one core reason. It turns men into passive beings. The sexual dynamic cannot exist between a couple where both partners are passive. One needs to be the dominant partner, and this needs to be the man. Women may be able to fill this role temporarily, but it will leave them exhausted and unsatisfied, without really knowing why.

TRANSGENDERS IN PORN

What is the relevance of talking about transgenders in this book? We will cover this phenomenon quite extensively, although we could cover it in far more detail. However, that may deviate too far from the core message of this book. Transgenders are a controversial topic that many have an opinion about, but few have any knowledge about. Who needs knowledge when you already have an opinion? We are going to focus on the link between the rising amount of transgenders and porn, a direct consequence of the passive approach men take and the fact that they feel related to the female performer on screen.

In porn it may be a niche, a relatively small market, but it exists nonetheless. In recent years the transgender idea has been pushed forward across the world. Transgender bathrooms became a topic of global importance. Should women that were born as men use the male bathroom as they had all their lives, or should they be allowed to use the female bathrooms? Shock and despair spread the nation and the world, surely it would be unsafe to let a person with a penis into the girls' bathroom? Beyond that, the discussion took place on what should legally define someone's gender. Can people legally change their gender on their passport?

"The sex listed on a person's birth certificate, as originally issued, shall constitute definitive proof of a person's sex unless rebutted by reliable genetic evidence."

- Memo by the Department of Health and Human Services

Whichever bathroom they use, many people struggle to understand transgenders. We're going to outline a controversial theory, linking the rise of transgenders to porn. The desire for many young men to turn themselves into women, is a fetishized behavior caused by relating to the female actress in porn movies. Their desire is not to be female, but to become sexually desirable.

This is the case for those that experience transgender feelings later on in life, after they have been exposed to pornography (and likely developed an addiction to it). Although this may not cover all transgenders, we do believe it covers a significant percentage of transgenders and forms an explanation for the fast increase in the number of transgenders. If any man has developed gender dysmorphia from consuming porn, it needs to be spotted and brought to the light to prevent this happening to other men. Due to the high suicide rate among post-operation transgenders, this is one way in which porn addiction could literally bring death. Confused young men believe they could be transgender, after which their doctor prescribes hormone altering medication. After taking this medication they obviously feel more like a woman, as they have more female hormones in their bodies. An odd case may make the step towards the operation, only to regret it afterwards. Since there is no way back, suicide is the only option for these men. And it all would have started with a porn addiction.

You may disagree with the hypothesis that is stated above, or you may accept it. Do we know for sure that this hypothesis is correct? No, otherwise it would not be a mere hypothesis. Unfortunately, we can't really research this topic. No university would even allow such research to take place, all of them are too afraid of being called out for it. They would be transphobic, a newly made up word. Regardless, every theory always starts out as a theory, until it is proven and becomes accepted as fact.

Despite this, it was not too long ago that transgenderism was considered a mental illness. It was only in 2018 that the WHO, the

World Health Organization, decided to no longer classify it as a mental disorder, after being pressured by activist groups. We will try to explain the logic behind the hypothesis though, and perhaps it will make sense. Before we get there, we need to talk about watching pornography with transgenders in there - probably the closest porn can bring you to thinking about changing your gender yourself.

Excessive consumption of porn leads to new horizons, the porn user needs continuously increasingly extreme material. These types of videos will only be watched by the more veteran porn users. The ones that have seen it all. The ones that need more and more to keep their erection firm. The ones that no longer get aroused from vanilla porn, or lesbian porn, or even group sex porn. They need something newer, something stranger to spark their interest. Frankly, this group consists of a very large portion of men.

They want to see women with dicks. Or men with tits. Whichever terminology you prefer. I suppose both descriptions are no longer allowed, as according to left-wing activists they are just as much a woman as anyone that was born as a woman. Whatever naming convention is in use, changes nothing to the nature of the being.

Transgenders in porn are almost never post-op. Meaning the actors are never post operation. Which operation do we refer to here? The one that removes the penis and replaces it with an artificial vagina. Or, the reverse, turning a vagina into an artificial penis. Female to male transgenders are however such a small niche in porn that it would probably be difficult to find a video of it even when desperately searching. Perhaps this will change, but I would not be able to explain to you why anyone would want to watch a male-looking person with a vagina have sex with a man. Not beyond the initial curiosity that this could trigger. There is really only one performer in that category, and that is Buck Angel. We'll talk more about these operations in a little while and it will become clear why these post-operation transgenders never appear in porn.

We don't talk much about female-to-male transgenders. They seem to be a lot rarer compared to male-to-female transgenders, not only in porn, but in real life too. The women that do feel like they are transgender, are often obsessed with male strength and building muscle. Some theories say that trauma has caused them to admire the strength and desire to become hypermasculine, to be better able to protect themselves. In some cases, the desire is followed by a traumatic abuse, or rape. One woman that turned into a man and had her breasts, ovaries, and uterus exchanged for a fake penis described her regret it in the following way:

'I'm a woman I'm not meant to be a bloke. I'm trapped. It's a complete mess - where do you even start? I just regret the decision. I'm sure a lot of transgender men feel the same too but I'm the only one honest and brave one to come out and say it. Mr. Harries [Debbie] says he feels 'mutilated' and believes he had the surgery because he thought if he did not have a vagina anymore he could not be raped.''

- Debbie Karemer

While male late-onset transgenderism may be caused by porn fetishism, for women it is more likely to come from such traumas like rape. Shockingly, these issues are not spotted during the initial psychological checks and people are pushed towards surgery.

The transgenders in porn videos can have sex either with women or with men. You might think that transgender on female porn is more popular, but some transgenders take so many hormones that they can barely get hard. This can make it difficult to find one that is suitable for such a scene. In other cases, when they can get hard, it is simply a bit odd to watch a feminine looking man have sex with a woman. Still, it appeals to some.

''Porn with transgenders gives you more to look at. Instead of a man fucking her, it's another 'woman' with a feminine face and tits!''

- Anonymous

This exact same person made the following comment later on in the conversation.

''I've been thinking about a MFM [Male-Female-Male] threesome with my girlfriend, I think it would be hot to watch her suck another man's dick.''

- Anonymous

This anonymous commenter just happened to be a fan of transgender porn, while at the same time developing a cuckold fetish. When speaking to him later on, he admitted he was happy never went through with this threesome. He was afraid that it would have ruined his relationship and that his interest in it was mostly porn-driven - the desire for the threesome vanished after he cut down on the porn for a few weeks.

Most transgenders appear to be more comfortable in the submissive role that gets penetrated. They are unable to broadcast this raw dominance when penetrating the woman. This transgender-on-female porn is the intermediate step, where curiosity and newness pull the viewer into it.

The viewer can justify watching it by following the logic that there is still a real woman in the scene. They simply replaced the male performer with a transgender. Since you are now viewing a woman having sex with a newly created woman, it is even more 'straight' than watching a man have sex with a woman. Or so you could make yourself believe. In reality, you are now eyeing a man with silicone implants while you orgasm, it would be difficult to explain how that would make it more straight than watching a single woman. Your brain is fully incapable of discerning the difference between silicone breasts on a male and silicone breasts on a female. Again, this absence of a relatable character in the scene destroys the ability to become a part of the scene in your fantasy. You cannot relate yourself to this transgender, so you take on a passive role of observing these two 'women'. Once more, you admit to your brain that you are a mere voyeur.

Strange as it is, a more common version is the transgender with a man. Usually, it will be the transgender that gets penetrated, though it can be the other way around as well. The version where the male gets penetrated, is more obviously homosexual in nature and less appealing. The transgender here takes on the submissive part, performing oral sex and receiving anal sex. They may jerk themselves off while being penetrated to reach orgasm as well.

The viewer has now descended into watching two male-born performers getting it on. The male brain nonetheless responds positively to these transgenders. The brain is tricked into believing you are watching a woman. Your rational brain knows that you are watching two men have sex, but your reptile brain doesn't care about this. The reptile brain does not recognize it. At this point, a straight male has reached the point where he is effectively viewing gay pornography and masturbating to it. No vagina is involved anymore.

The brain sees breasts. Hormones have created a more feminine allocation of body fat. Make-up covers the face and makes it look womanly. Your ancient brain cannot distinguish between this and a real female. It responds to these basic impulses. Maybe you can recognize that the breasts are fake, but if fake breasts on a woman still turn you on, then how would your brain tell the difference with fake breasts on a man?

The endless search for a novelty in porn, for something more taboo and more extreme, has now led the porn consumer to watch a video that really does not match their sexual orientation any longer. Assuming, of course, that the viewer was a straight male. Now in the current politically correct world, we need to put a caveat that if you acknowledge a transgender woman to be as much of a woman as a real woman, then by that logic the viewer is still watching very normal pornography. However, if we acknowledge that as nonsense, it is clear that the viewer is watching two people that were both born as men and both have a penis instead of a vagina. How did porn make someone's sexual orientation shift? At least, partially shift. We assume in real life these men are still attracted to women, although they may be more open to experimenting with a transgender, or even a man. They may easily start to fantasize at this stage, about sex with a transgender. Fantasies are always more of a safe place to start. This really means straight men fantasizing about touching someone else's penis and reaching orgasm with them. You may ask yourself how far removed from a gay fantasy that is.

Many viewers probably don't watch such videos because our rational brain still has some part in our decision making. Those that can stop and think about what they are doing, will likely decide against watching it. For porn addicts, this choice is not that easy.

Yes, porn can be addictive, as it is soon linked with this dopamine release in your brain. Not addictive on the scale of cocaine, but addictive on the scale of video games, or maybe even weed. Again a topic that not enough researched is done for, but other books have been written on the topic. As always, how vulnerable someone is to addiction depends on the person. Some people have become addicted to a video game like World of Warcraft, while others manage to casually consume cocaine without having major problems to stop using it when it does not suit their lifestyle anymore. The fact that porn is addictive is further shown by the massive amount of young men that are in healthy relationships with frequent sex, and still feel the need to masturbate to porn in the odd moment they are without their girlfriend. Surely, their libido had already been satisfied and porn is simply luring them in, like the irresistible call of the Sirens that drew sailors into their deaths. These men could be spending time in bed with their girlfriends, looking forward to the moment when they are alone again so that they can masturbate to porn.

A whole business has risen up around battling porn addiction. Well, if you have found yourself watching transgender porn, you should probably seek treatment for addiction. Regular porn has lost its appeal to you, and you have gone seeking deeper and deeper into the internet on finding something that can really give you that rush, that adrenaline shot. Not watching porn for a long period, several months to years, may make the less extreme material appealing to you again. A Playboy picture could become sufficient. At least temporarily, until you once more descend into the dark world of porn. The way to stay clean is to reject porn completely.

At this point, the viewer no longer cares about placing themselves into the fantasy. They may feel that they are not involved, simply a voyeur. Yet watching the videos could create impulses of fantasizing about sex with a transgender. This is a very slippery slope into gay fantasies, as you are fantasizing about sex with a man with tits. The penis is still there. Now, this can happen to men that have always been straight, but that fall too far into this hole of porn.

Once the viewer watches videos like this, they may start to imagine what it is like to take a cock into their own mouth. How would sperm taste? They may start to wonder how it would be to have something inserted into their ass. Since they are watching a video with two men, there is a character relatable to them in the scene. They can empathize with this transgender that is having sex with the man, and how he enjoys the acts. The transgender is at the core of the video. Suddenly all these questions no longer feel so repulsive and they cease to trigger a response of disgust in their minds. Their brain is changing.

They may even wonder how nice it would be to wear some female lingerie and turn submissive. They could experience this feeling of being sexually desired, a feeling unknown to many of them, yet always so appealing. Their homosexual fantasies will never be about dominating other men, it will always be about wanting to be taken by another man. This is obviously only applicable to those that have gone the furthest into the darkness. For men that have had no luck with women throughout their lives and are desperate for any sort of sexual relationship. They turn gay out of desperation, despite not really being attracted to other men, they are attracted to the idea of being desired by other men. Due to porn they may have even fetishized the penis, though not the male body and face. Hence why many transgenders claim they are still attracted to women, but are open to sexual activity with men regardless.

Our brains always copy what we see into our own minds. When we watch football, our brain unleashes the same hormones as if we would be playing football ourselves. Endorphins rush through our brain. There are not as many as if we would actually play football, but there are some, as significant amount. Our brains mimic what we see. Our brain sees exercise and it puts our mind in the same state, as if we were out on the field. This effect is not limited to watching football.

Imagine watching a sad movie, where the protagonist is experiencing lots of tragedy. You too will feel sad and moved, impacted by the story. You will relate to it - in fact, the best movies are the ones where we can relate to the protagonist. It even applies to someone telling you a story, and when you are emphatically listening to them. You may start to mimic in your mind the same feelings they are experiencing, this makes it easier for you to understand them. None of this has a long-lasting effect, your brain mimics a lot of different activities and stories during the day.

There is a difference when you spend many hours watching porn every week, you consume so much of it that it may start to leave a lasting effect on your personality.

Let's give one more example. Do you like hamburgers? Picture it in front of you. Feel it in your hands. Do you know how it feels when you take that first bite from the burger? That firm, warm brioche bun against your lips. That red, juicy meat unleashing the flavors into your mouth. Some sauce, not too much, not enough to make it all moist - the perfect amount of sauce while keeping the bun firm and easy to eat without dripping a lot. Some tomato and pickle, with their distinct flavors, rolling around on your tongue - mixing with the flavor of the beef. If you ever ate a burger and enjoyed it, reading this may trigger a certain response in your brain. In case it didn't have this effect, then take comfort in knowing that this usually works on people. It may have happened to you when you are hungry and you see others eat on television, that your mouth starts to salivate. It is that same effect.

This response is similar to what would happen if you actually would have this burger in your hands. And you may get a little happy, because you know you will soon receive those delicious calories that your body craves. Frankly, our bodies were not designed for modern opulence and therefore reward us for making sure the body doesn't starve. Lots of dopamine is released when eating that burger, the happy hormone that makes us feel good. Again, our bodies have not evolved over the last decades to adapt to a world where diabetes and obesity are a greater health-risk than starvation.

Now imagine a woman. Imagine her in a porn movie you have once watched. She is a blonde girl, with a big round ass. She bends over forward on the bed, sitting on hands and knees. She looks over her shoulder and gives you a cheeky smile. Fully naked. Her pussy is dripping juices and glistening with its moistness in the light. You are in the point of view of the male. Your dick is hard as you walk towards her. You put your left hand on her ass with a hard, firm, smack. With your right hand you take your cock and slide it over her pussy. You feel the wetness, the warmth. You push it all the way in and start fucking her.

Now, possibly, you started to fantasize about having sex with this girl. Perhaps we should have given you some more details to draw you in, but we believe we may have triggered something in you with just this. Some blood may have flushed to your face and your ears have got red just thinking about sex with this blonde girl. Let's try this once more.

Imagine a woman, at least, she looks like a woman. She is a brunette, with a big round ass. She bends over forward on the bed, sitting on hands and knees. She looks over her shoulder and gives you a cheeky smile. Fully naked. She is spreading open her ass for you, showing her tight, clean, asshole. A man comes in that starts to lick her ass. The woman moans. In between her legs you can see her balls and dick dangling down. She is jerking off while the man puts his dick inside of her ass. You are jerking off while watching. You start to think how it would feel to have something go into your ass.

What kind of response does reading something like this trigger in your mind? Maybe you felt some response, maybe not a lot, but this is only a single paragraph you read once. There are men watching hours of this material online - how long would it take for their minds to wander towards the unthinkable? Our brains all do the same when we are watching a man, even when it is a transgender, be submissive on camera and get fucked by other men. Moreso, the viewer will be observing all of this in a state of arousal. This is why we started with the paragraph about a real woman. This creates further links in your brain between what you are seeing and what arouses you. Your brain will start to make the connection. Watching a man with fake breasts gets linked to the dopamine-rush that is given upon orgasm. Soon, your body merely needs to think about transgenders and you will get turned on. You will become aroused because your body and mind have made this connection in the past. The only link your brain will have to transgenders is through porn and orgasm.

You may start to wonder what happens to your manliness, to your virility, your masculine dominance, when your brain makes connections like this. Even when you are not having homosexual thoughts or an interest in cross-dressing or changing your gender, does not mean you are as much of a man as you could be. Being a weak, both mentally as well as physically, man that is not getting the most out of life is nothing to be proud of.

The reason then that we cover transgenders so extensively is because it is the most extreme example of a man completely rejecting his manliness. Porn here has gone so far that not only does it weaken someone's masculinity, it has made them actively hostile against their own masculinity. Somehow in our modern culture, being manly has lost its sensation of pride. All porn flows into this direction, it makes men weaker and less of a man, but none of it, not even cuckoldry, goes as far at rejecting it as transgenders. It actively seeks to embrace femininity, the absolute opposite of masculinity, and something that these men can never attain. This we will cover in the next chapters, where we highlight that such surgery is no solution for these men.

We are talking about porn inducing transgenderism. This does not imply that we try to prove that all transgenders are brought into existence by excessive porn usage. Frankly, we don't know what causes men to want to change their gender. Until 2018 it was thought to be a mental disorder that required medication and psychological analysis to cure, according to the WHO. Now, saying it may be a mental disorder, caused by whatever it may, is borderline hate speech. What we can observe is that the amount of people that identify as a different gender appears to be rising in recent years, at the same time as global porn consumption has been rising. We also know that there is little research done on how these two could possibly be connected.

It does not mean that it has to explain all cases of transgenderism. Many may have other causes, but even if a tiny subset of those that become transgender, especially at a later age, that can be linked to porn usage, that would be a major breakthrough. Evidently, it would be much more comfortable for these men if they could be happy inside the bodies they were born in. They, like many other porn consumers, need to rediscover their virility.

On a closing note, it is also odd that there seem to be so many more men that feel they are transgender, compared to the number of women. And many of these men turn into hypersexual creatures, especially while they still have their penis. It is an unexplained difference in occurrence, but we do all know that men watch more porn than women.

THE TRANSGENDER EXPANSION

When a man has spent so many hours, so many orgasms, watching porn, what happens to their mindset? For so long, they have taken a passive approach, they have watched while others had sex. They have watched while women were pleased. They have watched while transgenders were pleasured. What we will discuss here is a very small risk, which most men will avoid with ease. Still, we see more and more male-to-female transgenders appear. Vastly more uncommon a decade ago, suddenly everyone seems to know someone that identifies as transgender. They seem to pop up everywhere you look.

We must dive into the link between excessive porn usage, and the desire to change gender. Men that identify as transgender are often excessive consumers of porn. They do so due to their lack of success with actual women. You could say they are involuntarily celibate, a situation the internet has coined as 'incel'. These men are completely undesired by the other sex. These men lack the confidence, the virility, to chase the other sex. That is not to say that it only applies to involuntarily celibate men, some men transition even while having a girlfriend and some even manage to remain in that relationship. At least temporarily, their actually female partners will soon grow bored of this arrangement.

Their desire for change is not driven by a desire to appeal to men. It is not driven by homosexuality. It is driven by the desire to be desired, as they see women are. They even want to desire their own body, they fetishize themselves. Their life is driven by the pursuit of what they lack most. Sex and intimacy. Foolishly, they believe sex will be easier to obtain once they are a woman.

Their porn consumption does not relinquish their thirst, but increases it. Like dangling meat in front of a dog, but keeping it out of reach, the dog will start to drool. The dog will become utterly focused on this piece of meat. The dog will become obsessed with this meat. So do these men become obsessed with sex. Porn is not a substitute for sex, but merely an appetizer. Many men consume this appetizer without ever getting to the main course, they are taken hold by a perpetual state of hunger.

They enter the stage of hypersexuality. An unnatural state for people to be in. A state that shows the addiction and blocks them from living the rest of their life. They are a slave to their passions. This is not to be confused with having a high libido. A higher libido can be a natural state, due to high testosterone. Hypersexuality is more similar to addiction, where the orgasm provides the 'high'. It implies a constant search for the next orgasm. One symptom may be the near-constant fantasizing about sexual acts. It is obsessive and places a burden on the other activities in their lives.

Over time, these men have started to identify with the female actors they have been watching. They adore them. They envy how they can be so passive and simply have another man give them sexual satisfaction. This submissive mindset takes over. All the women need to do is dress sexy, act flirty, and lay back. In their submissive mindset, the men consider this to be the ideal. The world is unfair to them for not granting them the same benefit. They believe they are inferior as men, compared to this higher status that the female has in their mind. They envy women. This view on status is a direct result of worshipping the female pornstars that they have bonded through by orgasming to their videos over and over again.

What do they do? They will start with wearing female lingerie. This helps them with their sexual roleplay. At this stage, it does not matter whether they identify as straight or homosexual. They go into their role of simply looking pretty, and being desired. They will seek out other, desperate, men to compliment them. Rather than having to chase, they can now be passive. Even if they attract men with it, instead of the women they desire. Yet, their submissive mindset does not end here. Some of these men admit that their transgenderism started with crossdressing. One user on a transgender forum said this:

''I just came out to my wife as transgender, she knows i dress as a woman occasionally, but this is the first time I said it to her out loud.''

They will seek out men online, or in real life, to submit to. They want to feel this desire from the other man. In return, they are happy to take on the role of the submissive woman. They want to be commanded. They want to somehow humiliate themselves. Like women, they want to be sexually used. Since they are unable to obtain sex being dominant, they swing the other way.

For some, it will stay at fantasizing, but others will go for the meet-up. The inbetweeners may search for online contact, where they can share pictures of themselves in lingerie with other men and receive compliments in exchange. In other cases, this will spiral into a meet-up, probably fueled by a binge on porn consumption and a hyper-aroused state after consuming hours and hours of porn without proper release. They will perform homosexual acts despite being more attracted to women. Their pleasure comes from submitting, the other person involved is less relevant. This is the result of the decade-long indoctrination from watching porn and identifying with the woman. After undergoing such an activity even once, the guy will start to have a serious internal discussion about his sexual orientation and sexual identity.

Sexual pleasure in their brain has gotten linked to being submissive. Of course, these are not yet our transgenders. These men are transvestites or cross-dressing homosexuals. Nonetheless, this movement towards swapping genders clearly shows us the hypersexuality present in this group. Undoubtedly transgenders start off as transvestites and cross-dressers. Suddenly, they will say they became aware that they have been denying themselves their true gender identity. It is only over time that they fully embrace their new gender identity, but its roots were in a fetishized behavior focused on sex. This is the key that we need to remember - their playful move towards identifying as a woman is rooted in a sexual role-play, their fetish became to pretend to be a woman. It is this fetish gone haywire that makes them want to extend this roleplay into every facet of their lives.

Transvestites are not interested in dressing as a woman, they are interested in dressing as a sexually appealing woman. Tight clothes. Short skirts. Sexy lingerie. Showing off their fake tits. None of them are interested in wearing a female hoodie and female skinny jeans. This does not provide them the same satisfaction. No, transvestites are purely sexual creatures. It is a fetish, similar to being a furry. Women may enjoy an au naturel look without makeup, but these men will put on makeup as if they are working as a prostitute. Their view of women is fully sexualized. They may not stand out in a dark nightclub, but in daily life they will not 'pass'. They only fit in, in a highly oversexualized environment.

The proper term for fetishizing your own, newly female, body is autogynephilia. It refers to being aroused with oneself. It appears to be common in those that identify as transgender after succumbing to porn addiction. One transgender describes the desire in the following way:

''I spent many years dreaming about (my vagina), imagining how it would feel to reach down and discover an opening, to feel right. I had sexual dreams about having a vagina from my teenage years onward. I dreamed that a hand would slide into my knickers and find a moist slit. That a finger would push in and then a phallus – plastic or real, would push in slowly and deeply and make me gasp. I carried on dreaming that dream until the night before surgery. The same faintly naive dreams that my vagina would work like any natal females. My surgeon told me he would make me look realistic, with a vaginal opening, a sensate clitoris and lips; inner and outer. I was told I couldn't have sex for at least three months. For 4 days after surgery, I didn't have sex dreams as I fell in and out of morphine-consciousness. I only wondered what my vagina would look like once the packing and bandages had come off. People post photographs but they tend to be the 'butterfly' ones. "Look at me," they say "I'm a beautiful pussy fuck me."
''

It is all overtly sexual, and it sounds as if the man is describing that he wants to be a girl in a porn movie. There is no desire to be a woman in daily life, it is fully about sex. They sexualize their own body, they truly become vain like Narcissus. They are obsessed with admiring their own body. Since many of these men are still straight, they enjoy observing their new female bodies.

Some may claim transvestites existed in the past as well. Many websites and books are dedicated to prove this, to thereby also prove that this is a perfectly natural phenomenon. This could be the case, but these transvestites often did not do so out of pleasure or personal will. These older forms were poor boys desperate to make a living. They were recruited into male-brothels and made up to look like women to attract a certain type of customer. That is not to say sexual deviancy did not exist back then, but we must recognize the difference between desperation and desire. An example of the type of brothel we are talking about here is shown in the Netflix show 'The Alienator' and covers the murders of such whore-boys. A similar situation still exists in Afghanistan today, where poor boys whore themselves out to older men. The boys will dress up as women and dance in a feminine way. The Afghans have a saying that 'Boys are for fun, women are for children'. The Taliban seeks to eradicate these behaviors, but it is common in many areas in the country.

This is very different from the current situation with 'Desmond the Amazing'. His real name is Napoles and he was declared 'gender-neutral' as a baby by his mother. He is a ten-year-old transgender boy that also happens to be a drag queen. It is basically a young boy dressing up as an overly sexualized woman and this is applauded as great progress. He danced on a stage in a gay nightclub called 'Whoa!' while being dressed in drag. He went around collecting tips from adult gay men, walking up and down the bar. He has become a favorite of the LGBT movement and frequently shows up in the news at gay pride parades or at other events where the boy is surrounded by gay men. Obviously, we would not expect this boy to be influenced by porn, but it does highlight the oversexualized cult of transgenderism, and the strange idea that we should take children seriously when they wish to change gender instead of protecting them. The boy is most likely either indoctrinated or abused. Although in the past we recognized that such boys were whored out due to poverty and desperation, now we feel this behavior is a sign of progress.

Transgenders go a step beyond transvestites, but still bears some resemblance to the other. Hypersexuality is also common among the transgenders. Even when they are not very promiscuous, which happens more by lack of interest from others than by their own volition, their mind is about feeling desired and looking appealing. They crave sexual attention. They simply take it one step further, from a part-time to a full-time activity. Their identity has become linked to their desire to be a woman. Gay or straight, either can make the move towards transgender and some skip the transvestite phase completely. The drag queens are of course rather flamboyant, and this does not suit the anxious porn consumer, so that scene is more likely restricted to homosexuals. That does not mean that they do not start to try on 'cute' girly outfits to see how they look in it - that act alone, even in the privacy of their own bathroom, makes them a transvestite. Yet, look at the quote below from someone wondering if - and speaking to a therapist about it - they are transgender. The quote below is taken from a forum for transgenders.

''*If I were watching porn I would put myself in the woman's place. Generally it's just been in a sexual context or wanting to look attractive. I've always put women up on a pedestal and they always held power over me emotionally.*''

It is interesting to pause here or a second to raise the topic of the Asian ladyboys. A well-known and common form of transgenders, ladyboys can be either transvestites or have some surgery done to have fake boobs. Rarely, if ever, would they have their penis removed. They generally prefer to simply tuck it in to hide it.

Though, many even don't have fake boobs, they simply wear a padded push-up bra to make it look like they have a small cup size. A not uncommon feat in most of Asia. Now, many of these men are working as prostitutes. Whole streets in big Asian cities are populated by ladyboys walking the streets, harassing tourists and offering their services. The question arises if these men are actually transgenders, or if they have found a niche market to make a living. Or, in some cases perhaps both.

Do they resemble the western transgenders of today, or the western boy-prostitutes of the past? The reality may be a combination of both. The ones that do have silicone implants show a greater commitment to their being transgender, but others may simply be too poor to afford it. We should be able to distinguish these groups between those that dress up as women during the night to attract customers, and those that dress as women any time they go out. The first group, that dresses up solely for customers, holds a resemblance to these old brothels filled with young boys that were forced to dress as women. It is a destitute poverty that brings people to such actions, and not a result of open-minded progressiveness.

The ones with silicone implants obviously fall into the second category. Would we see that even the second group of silicone-implant carrying ladyboys is highly over-represented in prostitution? Why would this be? Is it because they cannot find other jobs? Although some employers may discriminate, ladyboys are so common in this part of the world that it would be doubtful they cannot find a job anywhere. It would be very doubtful to say that all of them are driven to this job out of desperation and the inability to find any other sort of job.

Realistically, most men and women would take literally any

job before going into prostitution. Some women that are interested in the easy money are the exception rather than the rule. And the number of women that work as prostitutes that had that job as a childhood dream will be an even tinier percentage. It is after all rather demeaning to be a street walking prostitute that has to offer her services to all that come by. For most women, this is a nightmare scenario, not too far distanced from experiencing continuous rape.

What can we say about these ladyboys then, when we observe that both groups are highly overrepresented in the prostitution sector? We must conclude that as a whole the ladyboys, both silicone-filled and silicone-free, are hypersexual.

Their primary reason to exist appears to be to chase sexual satisfaction. All of them seem to be attracted to men. All of them are homosexual and found a way to attract a greater variety of foreign men by dressing as a woman. The market of straight men visiting prostitutes in Asia is a bigger market than that of gay men looking to have sex with Asian men. Often they engage in sex in a submissive manner, providing oral and receiving anal. Their desire is to sexually surrender.

Their vision of what a woman is, is based on the hypersexual image of women that porn portrays. After all, porn portrays only that single aspect, and that is the only aspect of being a woman that they desire to copy. It is this hypersexuality that attracts the tourists to use their services. To the ancient brain of the tourist they look like women, but they are 'women' that will never say no.

Women that will engage in all the depravity that these men seek to experience. The appeal in the ladyboy is not that they have a penis. Their customers are not homosexuals. Their appeal is in their willingness to participate in the kind of filth that a normal woman would say no to. That is combined with a porn driven fetishization of anything that is different. Female prostitutes are more often driven by easy money and desperation, they have no interest in fulfilling every wicked desire that the male customer comes up with. The ladyboys take pleasure in this, and some will go onto dating sites and seek to meet up with men to engage in such acts for free out of their own desire.

This last point truly proves their hypersexuality. Go on any dating app in South-East Asia and you will find one ladyboy for every ten women that you come across. Or even more, provided that you can spot them. It may be difficult to tell from a well-angled photograph. The transgenders will soon offer sexual services, for free or for money. They appear to think of nothing beyond sex. There is no interest in going on a dinner date. They are obsessed with having sex with new men all the time, it is no wonder that STD rates are significantly higher in this group than in the rest of the population. Due to there being no risk of pregnancy, many avoid using protection altogether.

If transgenderism is simply genetic, then how is it possible that it seems to be much more common in that region of the world than in the Western hemisphere? Why do we celebrate such behavior? Is it really the case that simply more people are unafraid of showing the world who they really are, or is there a different underlying cause driving this behavior. Is it simply submissive gay men that find it easier to transform into a woman? Is it with the physical build of an Asian man easier to have an appearance as feminine?

On a different note, if the amount of ladyboys is due to Asian homosexuals finding it easier to live as a woman, instead of as an effeminate gay man, then should we conclude from that that transgenderism is a logical extension and hidden craving for all effeminate gay men? Is the sudden surge of transgenders simply a group of gay men that move onto a logical next step? What does it mean that these men keep their penis? Is it simply that they cannot afford the surgery, despite wanting it, or do they feel no need, no desire even, to rid themselves of their penis? If they are happy with their penis, should we say they are experiencing true gender dysmorphia or are gay men that dress as women not classified as gender dysmorphic? How can we distinguish between all these different preferences?

Clearly not all transgenders are effeminate gay men. It may explain some of the numbers, but overall we see many, many men that turn to transgenderism were very regular straight men before they turned to taking female hormones and undergo surgery. All sorts of men seem to become transgender, the only aspect they can admit they have in common with one another is their affinity for porn.

SURGERY OR MUTILATION

There are men that say they feel like they are a woman trapped inside a male's body. This is how they feel. That they feel this way, does not make it true. It does not make it so that the best course of action is to undergo surgery. We have fallen very low if discussion on this topic is so limited as it is today. Even hinting at the current course of action being wrong, will only give you public assault. Bigot, racist, misogynist. Even the terms that are not really relevant for the transgender discussion will be used to insult you, if you even hint that we should have a discussion. Before you know it, you are called a National-Socialist, or Nazi. We should reconsider what we are doing at the moment and if the current course of action actually makes the most sense. There are plenty of reasons to believe that these people have mental issues, the quote given here below is a small indicator of that. The quote is given by Charles Kane, the person of interest in the BBC documentary called "One Life: Make Me a Man Again". He experienced regret after undergoing male-to-female reassignment surgery. Kane had stated he only wanted to become a woman after he had had a nervous breakdown.

"When I was in the psychiatric hospital, there was a man on one side of me who thought he was King George and another guy on the other side who thought he was Jesus Christ. I decided I was Sam.[Sam is the female name he chose for himself]"

- Charles Kane

This chapter will draw attention to the insanity of transgender reassignment surgery. If transvestites and hypersexuality can be caused by excessive porn consumption, and even someone's sexual orientation can shift by this search for new types of porn. Well, then porn can be the leading cause for people to undergo such surgery. How horrendous it would be if this supposedly 'no harm done' consumption of pornographic material leads to people making life-changing decisions. If excessive drug use would lead to people desiring to self-mutilate, would we not want to stop them, help them, and get them off this drug? We must ask the question; is porn so different? For those that believe the comparison to self-mutilation is wrong and poorly chosen, continue reading to understand more about the details of such surgery.

This surgery cannot be turned around. It is irreversible. Once it is done, it is done. You'll never be the same again. Doctors will say that it is a necessity for their mental health. Mentally, these people feel that they are in the wrong body. They feel that their penis is a constant reminder that they are in the wrong body. Removing their penis and constructing a neo-vagina, should help them solve this.

There is a matter of doublethink present in the transgender belief. Doublethink is an Orwellian term taken from the dystopian novel '1984'. It means that a person can hold two, or more, contradictory beliefs simultaneously, without admitting that they are mutually exclusive.

For example, these men must wear sexy female clothing in order to feel like a woman. Yet, a woman can still feel like a woman in baggy male clothing. The woman should not feel pressured to wear sexy clothing just to feel like more of a woman, it does not matter. These two statements cannot both be true. If the second is true, it means the men don't need to wear sexy female outfits. If the first is true, it would mean that women should feel less womanly when they wear a simple outfit. Yet, in modern life, both of these statements must be acknowledged to be true.

There are more. One, a transgender man that has not undergone surgery and still has a penis, is just as much of a woman as any real woman out there. Two, to truly feel like a woman, the transgender man must undergo surgery to complete his transition.

One, women with a small cup-size are women nonetheless. Two, transgender men should receive silicone implants to feel more like a woman.

One, women that have low estrogen and high testosterone are still women, because they have the XX chromosome. Two, men that are transgender should receive high estrogen doses to lower their testosterone so that they can be more like women.

We could go on and on like this. Any rational thought is missing from the topic and any real discussion is shut down.

This surgery is for men that often are already cross-dressing and even taking female hormones. Well, it is rather obvious that when you take a lot of female hormones that you will feel more like a woman, and thus feel more desire to take such a surgery. It is thus a vicious cycle that starts with cross-dressing, after which the doctor provides you with female hormones. Such hormones will obviously impact how you think. Charles Kane believes that the female hormones that he was prescribed to take influenced his decision-making process.

"I don't think there's anyone born transsexual. Areas of their human brain get altered by female hormones."

- Charles Kane

Researching transgenders after they have started taking female hormones is meaningless, as their body is already changing due to the hormones. No longer can any evidence be found of it being natural that they want to be a woman, as any result could have been caused by the hormones. These hormones will soon make them want to undergo surgery.

Doctors have been practicing with gender reassignment surgeries for a while. The example given below comes from dr. John Money that believed the mind is a blank slate and a child can be raised to be whichever gender we choose. John Money worked for the Johns Hopkins University.

David Reimer's penis was damaged when he was eight months old due to a circumcision gone wrong. Money believed a child had not developed a gender identity yet, and all of gender was a social construct that was developed later in life based on how others, such as the parents, would treat the child. Money therefore advised the parents to surgically alter David's appearance to be that of a female. David would become Brenda. For years, Money claimed the surgery had been a success. That was until at fourteen years old David Reimer began the process of becoming male again. He had not been satisfied as a woman. Years later David succumbed to depression, drug abuse and his eventual suicide.

In the United States, such reassignment surgeries began in 1966 and were performed by Elmer Belt. The best-known example of such reassignments taking place before that is in Weimar-Germany, however, this ended there with the rise of the National-Socialist Party. Lili Elbe was the first in Germany to undergo such surgeries, but died after the complications of a uterus transplant. These people were obviously not influenced by porn, but in recent years the concept of changing gender has risen to a level of prominence that it never held before.

We could wonder what it even means to be in the wrong

body, as there have always been girly men and manly girls. Neither was limited in their behavior and could act the way they felt comfortable, without having to undergo surgery to change their gender.

Back in the 1990's TV's were filled with shows about odd people. These shows would have people on that were tattooed to look like a tiger, or like a cat. Some would have their tongue split to look like a snake. Some would have their ears removed to look more like their earless spirit animal. Everyone acknowledged these people were crazy. Nowadays, people claim without hesitation that they are 'cross-species'. We may still consider these people crazy, but for how long? Will we need to acknowledge that people can identify as a cat and that reassignment surgery must be funded by the government? Recently a man applied to have his age changed in his passport, because he felt younger than he was. An episode of South Park already mocked this several years ago, in an episode where one of the characters underwent surgery to look more like a dolphin. Of course, after the surgery, he realized he could never be a real dolphin. Similarly, some transgenders come to this realization afterward. The quote below comes from the Guardian.

"My psychiatrist told me, you look great, you can pass. I've come to realize that human life is made up of connecting, not passing. I can 'pass' in a shop, I can 'pass' on the street. But when you tell a man your background, if you're lucky he'll walk away. Nothing can prepare you for that. I feel notorious in any group. You can say you're Napoleon but unless the whole world agrees with you, you patently are not Napoleon. I'm not a woman, I'm a thing - a chimera. As I move into my middle *years, I'm genuinely worried that I just don't fit anywhere."*

Some readers may find this comparison to transgenders to be one of poor taste. Yet not so long ago it was commonly accepted that your chromosomes determined your gender and it was as simple as that. Anyone denying their gender, or their chromosomes, was denying a basic element of nature. Someone with XY chromosomes claiming that they were a woman, was considered insanity. The fact that you had XY chromosomes was the definitive proof of being a man. The only way to be a woman, was to be born with XX chromosomes. This is what was stated in the biology books in school. Suddenly, gender has become fluid. The distinction between 'gender' and 'sex' is completely made up, the two are synonymous. Chromosomes don't seem to mean anything anymore. But if it is not chromosomes that make us male or female, if it is not our physical appearance, if it is not our having a penis or a vagina that determines our gender, then what does? The only thing left is how we feel inside our head. What gender do we feel that we are? In the modern world, it is all about feelings. But what gender we feel like we are, can that not be easily influenced? If the problem arises in our brain, do we usually not medicate or send someone to a psychologist?

Anyway, let us assume that these people are in the wrong body. Is surgery the answer to their problems? It sounds so pleasant, you go to the doctor with a penis and leave the hospital with a neo-vagina. Okay, you don't have a womb, but beyond that, you are now a real woman. Or, so we are supposed to believe. But how good is our surgery? Skip the next paragraphs if you don't want to visualize how this operation takes place.

We should believe surgery only takes place after a thorough psychiatric analysis, but let's read the following fragment from an interview with several transgenders facing regrets, taken from The Guardian.

"I was referred for surgery after one 45-minute appointment. The emphasis was on one thing - my appearance. My motives for wanting the operation were never explored. The psychiatrist asked the most general questions. Did I play with dolls, did I have a strong male role model. There was no interest in the life I lived or how I made a living. Now I'm living on my own in a council flat. This is the last place I ever wanted to be."

The 54 year old Rowe believes his diagnosis as a transgender was wrong, as he was suffering from severe depression and had recently experienced multiple traumas in his life, culminating with his mother's death. How does he describe his current situation?

"Trapped between male and female."

- Rowe

Dainton suffered all her life with rejection issues due to being given away for adoption as a baby. This mental issue was worsened when her adoptive mother passed away. She decided not to discuss this during her conversations with the psychiatrist, as she felt it would slow down the process of getting towards gender reassignment surgery.

"I expected the surgery to solve those anxieties about my identity and when it didn't, I began to wonder whether I'd done the right thing."

- Dainton

Helen, who now is called Finch, wonders why people take gender reassignment requests so serious. We do not provide help to anorexic patients that want to be skinnier by providing them a liposuction.

"The fact that someone's suicidal and wanting something isn't a reason to provide it. The analogy I use about giving surgery to someone desperate to change sex is it's a bit like offering liposuction to an anorexic."

- Helen

Also, take note that there is no way back. Surgeon James Bellringer admits that there is not much he can do for someone that regrets changing their gender. He has performed over 200 sex changes in the last four years, so he clearly has experience in the field. In his words, any attempt to reverse the surgery would result in a mess.

"The erectile tissue has been taken out, so you need a prosthetic. The urethra is gone,

so you'd have to construct one out of a tube of skin. The tip of the penis will have been made into a neo-clitoris and I don't think you could put it back in its original place. It would probably be at the base of the artificial phallus. It's a mess."

- Surgeon James Bellringer

To understand why reversal is so difficult, let's have a look at the process of turning a man into a supposed woman. The 'meat' of the penis is removed, while the skin of the penis is folded inwards. This skin forms the brand new vaginal canal. This skin has hair growth, as hair can grow at the bottom of the shaft of the penis, and on the shaft to some degree as well. This means, first of all, that hair can keep growing inside this new vagina and even that a hairball can form inside if it is not cleaned regularly. Due to the origin of the skin, this hair growth will persist and will not eventually simply stop. Quotes below taken from an article from the Guardian on transgenders with regret.

''It was horrible, I'd created a monster. One day I was making love and something didn't feel right. There was this little ball of hair in my vagina."

"It's made of skin that's meant to be on the outside of the body that's now scuffed and crusty."

"Their language is illusory. You fundamentally can't change sex. The surgery doesn't alter you genetically. It's genital mutilation. My 'vagina' was just the bag of my scrotum. It's like a pouch, like a kangaroo. What's scary is you still feel like you have a penis when you're sexually aroused. It's like phantom limb syndrome. It's all been a terrible misadventure. I've never been a woman."

There is no natural lubrication of this new vagina. Arousal will not open it up, nor lubricate it. The body treats this new vagina as an open wound that it constantly tries to heal. Post surgery, these transgenders need to 'dilate' their vagina. Dilation means inserting a phallic object to reopen the wound. They need to do this ideally every single day to prevent the wound from slowly closing and them losing 'depth' in their vagina. As the wound would close gradually, losing depth means the deeper inside is healing and you won't be able to insert anything into it that deep anymore. Regaining depth would require extra surgery, after which the transgender would need to dilate again, daily, for the rest of their lives.

Is there no lubrication at all? No, there is some. Puss can leak through, as it is an open wound. In some cases, a connection is made and urine or liquid coming from the intestines can leak out through this vagina. To keep clean clothes, these transgender women have their own version of a period every single day the rest of their lives. Every day they need to wear pads to prevent this puss from getting into their clothes.

When they do engage in sex, there is no self-lubrication. The skin on the inside is that of the shaft of the penis, different from the skin on the inside of an actual vagina. There is also no natural absorption of sperm inside this new vagina, so everything that goes in, must come out. You can try searching for pictures of such new vaginas, and see if they even look the same on the outside. You may consider if it looks very appealing to you.

Even regular urination can bring more problems to the transgender, depending on how well the surgery goes. If the ending of the urinary tract is poorly angled, it can even be difficult to urinate in a toilet while sitting down without spraying it over the toilet seat and floor.

It is said that suicide rates in the transgender population are above average due to bullying and lack of acceptance from their community, although this can of course not be proven. We should wonder how many commit suicide out of regret. You can find blog posts online written by transgenders that deeply regret undergoing surgery and mutilating their perfectly fine penises.

The question we must ask here is; is this surgery really the end-all fix-all to their problems? Will this bring them ease at heart? Will it bring them satisfaction? Is it not a mere Fata Morgana, a mirage, make-believe, that this will help them? Will they really feel like more of a woman in their mutilated bodies? Will their anxiety really subside?

And if they do, are they really satisfied or are they fooling themselves? After this surgery the transgender has two options. Regret and depression, likely followed by suicide. Or, acceptance and an outward display of satisfaction, even if this requires them fooling themselves. Even if it means living in constant denial that what they did was equal to mutilating their body. It is one or the other.

Should we really be proud of our 'progressive' stance towards transgenders? We may be proud of not shunning people that experience such inner struggles and who feel this way in their heads. Such tolerance is a unique trait. However, there is more to it than mere tolerance. We should not feel proud of pushing them towards surgery. We should not be proud of saying to them that we have a solution to all their problems, simply undergo surgery and you will feel better. We will take your problems away. Those are mere lies.

As a society, we are not truly bothering to help these people. We offer them one solution and want to feel as if we have done the right thing. That these people end up killing themselves later on is out of sight and out of mind. Even when they do commit suicide, the general reply is that it must be due to ostracization from the rest of society, despite the many known cases of men simply regretting to have mutilated their bodies and knowing there's no way back.

Is the reverse any different? There are also female-to-male transgenders. They can receive a newly created penis. An even more challenging task, as something needs to be created out of nothing. Where does the skin from?

Gruesome as it may sound, the skin comes from their thighs, arms, or other body parts. The skin is peeled from arms and legs, to be molded into a penis. Without intending to offend anyone, it brings to mind the image of Frankenstein. Different parts of skin stitched together to create a neo-penis between the legs. The neo-penis is basically a stick of meat, somewhat resembling a penis. Meatstick may sound like a crude terminology, but what else should it be called? Certainly, it is not an actual penis. We could call it a synthetic penis made out of flesh that has almost none of its functionality.

For the head of the penis, skin from the inside of your cheeks can be used as this is more sensitive and soft. The penis cannot get erect, so what they create is a firm, rather large, stick of meat. An erection is impossible to obtain. The sensation of this penis would never be the same as a real penis, as it does not have the same sensitivity.

The vaginal lips are molded in the ballsack, which will generally be kept rather small and of course, it is fully empty. It is merely decorative. No sperm can be ejected from this new penis. It is doubtful if rubbing it could even result in an orgasm or if the clitoral head is still towards the base of the penis.

After extension, the urinary tract can reach the tip of the penis so that it can be used for that purpose. Again, you can search online for pictures of such creations. You may wonder if there will be any man or woman that would like to provide oral sex on such a penis. You may wonder if sex can be truly pleasurable for any side with such material.

Although medically impressive, we should consider if the people that undergo such surgeries have realistic expectations of the outcome. To what extent are they driven by despair, to what extent would these people attempt anything to fill this gaping void in their lives? The surgery, for all its purposes, appears to be a scam, a false promise. Does possession of such a synthetic dick really improve their quality of life? Was it really the one thing missing in their lives that they need to reach completion and satisfaction?

It is of course, shocking that transgenders, despite being such a minor, though growing, part of the population have such a reach in political discussions. We can see that for young people identifying as transgender, many of them simply grow out of this phase. They are influenced by how fashionable it is currently to be transgender. Something that makes you unique. Children especially, are easy to confuse in these topics.

A boy that enjoys playing with girls and with dolls may believe to be transgender when asked about it, and a girl that enjoys playing in the woods may feel she is more of a boy. Simply not conforming to gender stereotypes, does not mean you do not belong to that gender. And it should be no reason to start these children on hormone treatments, blocking their ascent into puberty. Most transgenders are, however, not identified in childhood, but only later on, after their exposure to porn.

We must remember that children, on most topics, are easily influenced by fads and they are rather ignorant. A child is not capable of making such a decision, and we should not expect it to do so. This is why children cannot vote or consent to sex. Hormone blockers for children truly are a form of child abuse. Yet in a country like Canada, refusing to allow your child to take hormone blockers could be considered to be a part of child abuse and contribute to your child being taken away by the government. It is the meek men that allow these things to happen. A child may feel it should eat candy all day, and be thoroughly sad when you don't let them do that. That does not mean that the feelings of the child are right. As a parent, you must know better. As a man, and a father, you must maintain your virility when raising your children and leading your family.

To summarize, it is possible that excessive porn consumption can lead to a submissive mindset and hypersexuality. This combination brings men to cross-dress. Those receptive to it may go one step further and begin to identify as transgender. A subset of that group may go for the surgery. But does this surgery really help them? A rhetorical question, as we have shown that this is in many cases not the case.

From a forum where porn addicts come together to fight against their inner demons, we take the following quote from a thread that discussed how these men felt porn was making them transgender:

''I identified hugely with the women in porn scenes and fantasized about being dominated.''

We see that men admit they identify with the women they watch in their porn movies. Moving beyond that, one user asked on an online forum filled with transgenders - they were either already on hormones, or undergoing surgeries - if they watched transgender porn. The answers were all 'yes'.

''All the time, but I thought it was a fetish. Every once in a while I would get really sad and google how to become a shemale. I didn't have any other word for it at the time, because my only exposure to trans women came through porn.''

- A deleted account

The quote above shows what we have posited here too, porn is influencing our society and what is depicted in porn spreads into the rest of our world.

''I did, but I always identified as the postop transwoman I was looking at.''

- hanazon0

Men identify with the person in porn that they are viewing. Obviously this also applies to transgenders when that is what they are viewing.

''I would dress and get myself off fantasizing I was the trans girl in whatever vid I was watching.''

- Alyssa_B

Again, a man that fantasizes about being the girl. They identify with who they watch.

''Trans porn is the only thing I masturbate to, it made me really want to become a trans girl.''

- Nordic Fairy

This is a transgender person that basically admits that watching porn, and specifically transgender porn, is what made them to be a transgender girl. This begs the question, would this person have felt as if they were a woman before? Or did identifying with the trans girls in porn create this desire?

''Yup, I got to the point of exclusively looking at it. I'm incredibly vain and aroused by my own self. I fetishize my own

transition from time to time, no idea if that's healthy or not.''

- Maleia

The note on fetishizing their own body is truly noteworthy. It implies these men are so addicted to porn, that they are turned on by turning into something that resembles the porn world - a transgender. A strong case of autogynephilia.

Another confused guy phrases it in the following way:

''I'll try to keep this as succinct as possible but bear with me cuz this is bound to take a bit of text. Anyway, backdrop first I am a 25 yo guy in a nearly 3 yr relationship and I do legitimately love this girl. Lately, however, I've been struggling with what i suppose is gender dysphoria. I'm struggling to figure out if this is rooted solely in a sexual fetish of some sort… or perhaps a symptom of something deeper I am subconsciously trying to suppress. I have been into sissy and transgender porn now for awhile, and it has been pretty much the standard for the past two years for me to imagine being in the female role whenever I masturbate.''

And another. The man questions whether his desire to be a woman is simply a porn-induced perversion or whether he is a true transcender. Nowhere does he imply that he had these desires before porn led him towards perversion.

''My thing is I get so aroused by these things [transgender porn] and I enjoy wearing feminine clothes both emotionally and sexually, so I'm really unsure if I'm just overtly perverted or whether I'm truly questioning my gender or not.''

This received a lot of positive replies along the lines of 'Why else do you think are watching transgender porn? Because you want to see people that are like you.' That, is completely ignorant towards the effect porn addiction can have on people. As a community, the transgenders did not warn these men that this was not a natural way to become transgender. Instead, they considered it a perfectly normal procedure to first watch a lot of porn, and then come to the sudden shocking realization that you are in fact a woman. The men in the comments found all these situations relatable, and encouraged the men to transition and take hormones.

Those with zero normal interest in this type of porn, may stumble upon it once they are desensitized to regular porn and suddenly find it interesting - even when at the start of their porn consumption they would have been repulsed by it. Some users are very aware that their gender confusion did not exist before they discovered their new fetish. This effect of porn does not seem to surprise anyone in the transgender community, nor does it trigger a halt in the prescription of hormones.

''I can't remember feeling any sort of

gender confusion before I discovered this fetish (but that doesn't mean I never did, I just can't remember). Sometimes I feel like (since the brain is plastic after all) the dopamine release associated with my fetish has rewired my sexual preferences and possibly even my true gender.''

Could we help people by attacking the root cause, by tackling this submissive hypersexuality? All of this finds the origin in modern porn. How would these men have turned out without it? Would they have discovered their inner virility? Perhaps this does not apply to all, and many transgenders will undoubtedly reject this conclusion, but the transgender may be led by cognitive dissonance and we cannot simply take their word for it.

When another poster described their current, confused, situation, many transgenders chimed in to say that this closely resembles what they felt themselves. What was the situation? A history of porn addiction and depression, leading the poster transgender porn and sissy hypnotic videos. They mentioned they felt romantically and sexually attracted to women, but had been posing in a skirt in front of the webcam and were curious about what it would be like to be a woman. This is the 'road to transgenderism' that many others could easily relate to. A road that starts in a desire to be desired, due to an identification with the women in porn.

If there is a subset of this group that is driven to this behavior by porn consumption, then it is a problem we must discuss and we must tackle. If we truly care about the people around us, we want to prevent them from committing such everlasting genital mutilation on their bodies. It is very suspicious, to say the least, that so many men are not aware that they are trapped in the wrong body until after they become addicted to porn and stumble upon transgender porn videos.

THE CUCKOLD

Transgenderism is by far the most far-reaching result of porn consumption, and just because you do not fall into that category does not mean that porn does not affect your masculinity. The same goes for cuckoldry, it is a more extreme result from a longstanding porn addiction.

The term finds its origin with the cuckoo bird, who lays its eggs in another birds nest. Despite the cuckoo not mating with the other bird, their eggs will be looked after by the other bird. Birds are apparently not that good at recognizing that the eggs are not their own. In the time of Shakespeare it meant that a wife had sex with other men, besides her husband, without the husband knowing. This could lead to the woman getting pregnant from another man, while her husband would think the child is his. Similar to the birds, the husband would be tricked into raising another man's child. Hence the comparison and the introduction of the terminology. Modern DNA testing has shown that this is still the case around 10% of the time. Ten percent of men are raising children they believe to be theirs, but really are not.

Nevertheless, the current meaning of cuckoldry is different. It is an old term that has been popularized in modern porn culture, and embraced as an insult by the right-wing. Cuck was used to describe any unmanly man, or left-wing supporter, and embraced for that purpose by the alt-right. In the fetish or porn scene, a cuckold is a man that enjoys watching his wife have sex with other men.

It is rather far-reaching to actually make it happen in real life, but for the men that do enjoy cuckoldry, its origin is likely in their porn consumption. In a sense, whenever you watch porn you are watching another man have sex with the girl you are attracted to. There is a thin line between this voyeurism and cuckoldry, and that line is who exactly the woman in the scene is. For a cuckold, this is their wife or girlfriend instead of a random porn actress.

You too, are on a path towards this behavior, depending on how susceptible you are to such ideas. That is, unless you have already stopped watching porn. Even if you never reach these stages, porn affects your masculinity, but that is a message that should be getting clear by now.

What is cuckoldry in porn? A cuckold is someone that takes pleasure in watching another man have sex with his wife or girlfriend. It is in this sense different from the voyeur, who watches strangers as they have sex. For the cuckold, there is a big element of humiliation. He has to stand idly by while his wife, his woman, gets fucked by another man.

It should not be compared to swingers or open relationships, because there both the man and the woman can have sex with others. Swinging is more common for old couples that are bored of having sex with each other after several decades, while many cuckolds are young men.

The cuckold merely observes. It's not a threesome, as he does not actively participate. Any participation that does take place is usually limited to further humiliation. For example, after the other man, the 'bull', has orgasmed inside the woman, the cuckold may be invited to eat her out. This emphasizes his submissive status, as he consumes the sperm the bull unleashed into his wife. In some cases the cuck may end up having sex with his woman, but only after the bull is finished. He needs to wait for his turn. In some cases, the cuck may not even be present, but he will be aroused from the stories his wife tells him of what she has done. She may send him photos while she is having sex with the other man, or send text messages or even call her boyfriend or husband. This way, even when he is not present, he can enjoy his humiliation.

Taking pleasure in this goes against all laws of nature. What men would want to observe another man - try to - impregnate his wife? It is fully, absolutely, counter-intuitive for anyone to take pleasure in this. It is incomparable with swinging or open relationships, as there both partners would engage in sex with others. There is a certain equality in that, while here the man is placed at the bottom. Perhaps the man will sit in the corner of the room jerking off, perhaps he is not even allowed this little pleasure. In some cases, the bull will sling insults towards the cuckold to extend the shame and humiliation. The cuckold feels comfortable in this roleplay. Nobody would imply that taking joy out of humiliation is a masculine trait.

Some cucks will argue that it is natural to get turned on by watching another man have sex with your wife. They use the same reasoning we shared in this book, namely that it is a biological trigger to watch another man and woman have sex, as your sperm can compete inside her. That is true and it explains why porn turns us on, but it does not make sense to be actively aroused by seeing this happen to a woman that is already yours. It is not logical to prefer sperm competition when it is not necessary. Moreover, sperm competition triggers feelings of anger, not pleasure. It prepares you to fight the other male.

On top of that, there is no humiliation involved in sperm competition. It is arousing because you will attempt to steal the other man's woman away. Cuckoldry has no natural basis, its foundation is a desire for humiliation and a feeling of inferiority towards both the bull and the woman. They feel that they deserve this humiliation, because they are not capable of sexually satisfying their woman. Instead of improving their sexual prowess, by practicing new techniques or working out at the gym, they prefer to feel sorry for themselves and bring in another man. They rather feel like the humiliated victim, than take control over their lives and fix what is wrong. That is the core of cuckoldry, sperm competition is a silly excuse.

Our hypothesis states that this fetish comes from too much porn consumption. The passive role that the viewer takes in porn is translated into the passive role the cuckold desires to take in real life. He is used to being a non-participating element in the act and has gotten comfortable in this role. His mind has started to equate sex and orgasm with watching others. His mind is so confused, that he will find watching porn more pleasurable than having actual sex with his wife. He would rather masturbate while watching others have sex, than penetrate a vagina.

He feels uncomfortable in the dominant role that is required in real physical sex. His mind is surprised by the feeling of a real vagina instead of the firm grip of his hand. The 'death grip' commonly used by men in masturbation will result in any vagina feeling rather not-so-tight. His performance in bed may be bordering on erectile dysfunction. Clearly, these men do not understand what the cause for their poor performance in bed is. Instead of finding the root cause, they embrace their incompetence.

All of this leads the man to be unable to satisfy his woman in bed. He knows this. Rather than believing he can improve his skills and become better, become more comfortable in his natural role, he feels he should avoid the act. He shies away and tries to recreate his porn experience.

Since his view of sex is based on porn, he feels emasculated. For years he has watched men with bigger dicks, and better bodies also, than himself. For years he has been frustrated, while watching these unattainable women have sex with other men. For years he feels he has been unable to satisfy his woman in the same way. Yet mostly, for many years he has not been able to take the same pleasure out of filling the dominant role in sex with his woman, as he takes out of masturbating while watching porn. His brain is fully adjusted to being an inactive witness to the act.

A cuckold's fantasy begins with the invitation of the bull. The man can watch a more dominant man give satisfaction to his wife. He may justify this in his mind by believing he is really doing his wife a favor here, by allowing her sex with the other man, but he is not granting her an open relationship. She cannot simply go out and meet other men for casual sex, while coming home to her loving husband. Even such an open relationship is based on a certain mutual respect and discrete behavior. Here, the woman can only have sex with other men if he is watching, or if she tells him about it and humiliates him with it.

Cuckoldry is very different from this open relationship. The cuckold is not interested in granting his wife more sexual liberty, no, he desires to watch. It is a selfish act, not an altruistic one. He wants to be involved in the act, although not physically. Some men will even push their unwilling wives into sex with the bull, claiming it will help their marriage and their sex-life. The reluctant wife will hear her husband beg to have sex with a stranger in front of him. Internet blogs are filled with questions on how to talk their wives into it. It is borderline emotional abuse, blackmailing the woman into sex with strangers against her own free will. The woman has to make a choice; save her beloved marriage and have sex with another man, or allow her husband's cuckold fetish to destroy the marriage. This is in a way delusional, any form of cuckoldry will destroy the relationship. The reality is that such a choice given to a woman is in essence a false dilemma. The moment a man becomes interested in cuckoldry, the relationship is effectively over. It is the nail in the coffin.

There will be men that have regrets afterwards. The reality differs from their fantasy. You cannot unsee another man penetrating your wife, there is no way back to the normal relationship that you were in before this event took place. If the man regrets it, he will be filled with a certain disgust for his wife.

She is no longer pure, no longer his, and despite him being the one that requested this act, he will grow to resent her. That same resentment will originate from the wife's side. How can she respect her husband any longer after seeing how he rejoices in the role of a pathetic loser that jerks off while a more masculine man is penetrating her? Even when the woman does not get a crush on the bull, it is likely to trigger the end of the relationship. These are not things that can be contained to the bedroom, and ignored outside of it. This becomes a defining element of the relationship. Sex is not a separated element of life, it is at its core.

What woman can love a man that asks her to fuck someone else? A woman's love for a man is more akin to respect, different from maternal love. She wants a man to look up to, to admire and adore. A man that deserves her devotion. A sad creature that takes joy from humiliation is hard to respect. Who respects a man that is begging you to have sex with another man? The woman will find herself feeling negative, full of resentment, about the man, never will she be able to show him the admiration that she has done before.

She may stay in the relationship out of fear for the unknown, out of fear of not finding another suitor and ending up alone, but she will not be happy. This fear mostly applies to the women that are a bit older, beyond their most fertile years. Even when the woman is open towards cuckoldry, she will start to feel more positive about the bull than about her husband or boyfriend. Every orgasm the bull gives her, unleashes oxytocin, a bonding hormone, in her mind. Sooner or later, she will grow feelings for the bull. This dominant, real man, that can satisfy her, versus the weak man that watches them. It is a very natural response to feel more positively about the dominant man. Cuckoldry is suicide to a relationship.

Some men counter this natural bonding between sexual partners by choosing a specific type of men as their bull. A man from which there is no risk for it to evolve into a relationship between the bull and the woman. This may be because the bull is significantly younger than the couple, and the bull would have no interest in the woman for anything beyond sex. It may be because the woman enjoys the company of more intellectual men and the bull is an ignorant brute. In some cases, couples will prefer to use a black man as a bull, as the woman will feel more hesitant to run away with a black man. At least, that is the logic used by the cuckold. This is part of the same racism present in interracial porn, where black men are viewed as having more sexual prowess, but also as lower and more animalistic. They counter the lack of respect the woman will feel for them, by using a bull that she will not be able to fully look up to either. Another strategy is to constantly change bulls, to avoid any feelings developing. It shows some recognition on the part of the cuckold, an awareness of the risks involved in this dangerous game. Yet, despite being fully aware of the risks, the cuckold still wants to live this fantasy. Addicts are not known for their self control, and cuckolds are porn addicts at the core.

Interracial porn and cuckoldry often go together. Sites such as 'Blacked' focus on the emasculation of the white man, implying it takes a black man to bring full satisfaction to the woman. The white man is weak and effeminate, submitting to its faith of being a sexual unsatisfactory reject. This ideology closely resembles that of the cuckold, who feels he is too incompetent to provide his woman with that pleasure. He needs the help of a more brutish creature. These cuckolds live in a cognitive dissonance where they will always deny their racism, perhaps believing that it does not count because they look up to black men. Porn has indoctrinated these men to believe that they are inferior to these other men. The biggest part of this inferiority, may be due to their own submissive mindset. If they would flip the switch to their dominant side, then they could provide this sexual pleasure themselves. Such cuckolds often take pride in their more intellectual nature. Sexually they may be inferior, but intellectually they are the superior ones. This allows them to further justify their cuckoldry, as the man, the brute, they are using as the bull is likely not intellectual. They feel this reduces the risk of their woman leaving them, as surely she values their intellect too much. Still, what barrier do these intellectual men have to being dominant in bed as well? There is no reason men cannot be both, in fact, men should be both. The modern dualist belief that men are either rude and muscular, or kind and intelligent, is a false dilemma.

For the man, as always, such fetishes originate in feelings of inadequacy. It is this Christian idea that sinners must receive punishment. It is similar to the flagellants of Medieval Europe. The idea is that, if you have sinned, you should punish yourselves. These men feel that they are not big enough, that they cannot last long enough, that they cannot perform the same way the men in porn do. All this inadequacy originates from too much porn consumption and taking that as a baseline to compare themselves to. It is then worsened by their lack of dominance, which is what turns women on most.

This inadequacy goes hand in hand with the submissive mindset. How can they make the woman feel desired, when they are submissive and passive themselves? The more insecure they become, the more passive, leading to even greater insecurity. They end up so passive that they prefer to remove themselves from the act of sex completely. This brings them into their comfort zone, the same zone they are in when masturbating to porn. Make no mistake, this removal from sex is not due to a lack of libido. They will jerk off eagerly and are closer to hypersexuality than to asexuality. Their lives are focused on getting their next great orgasm, mimicking the orgasms they can get from watching porn. For these men, sexuality is inherently linked to porn and not to the real act. Their addiction has pushed them towards hypersexuality, and they keep craving something new and more extreme to be able to masturbate to.

Other sources will tell you other reasons that cuckolds exist. They will say it offers a nice escape from their dreary existence, that it is simply another fetish that is part of the BDSM group. The men, so they say, simply enjoy the roleplay. They like the idea of being unable to satisfy their wife, driving her to have sex with others - as if this is merely a game they are playing, a game of pretend. These reasons are given as if they make perfect sense.

As if it is a natural fetish for men to enjoy another man have sex with their wife. As if this is just an interesting experience to be able to witness your wife have sex while you are reduced to being the audience. Of course a cuckold will not say that the fetish arose out of porn consumption and a passive mindset, of course they will provide other reasons that sound seemingly logical. But that does not make it true. An addict never admits they are an addict, for once they do admit to their addiction, they usually start to work on ending it. Especially once they recognize the harm it does to them.

Cuckoldry may be an extreme, but it is a relationship killer. At best the relationship stays intact, but what kind of position will the man have in this relationship? Will they really be able to contain the humiliation to the bedroom? Of course not. More likely this behavior stems from a desire to watch 'live porn'. It does not take them out of their comfort zone to become a cuckold, it places them right back into their comfort zones.

The more innocent form of cuckoldry is that of a threesome involving two men. This way the primary partner is still involved, but so is another man. It allows the man to become an observant of how, for example, his girlfriend is giving a blowjob to another man, yet without the humiliating roleplay that a cuckold adores so much. Still, it will be devastating for them to watch their girlfriend eagerly suck another man's cock and it will likely be the end of that relationship. Seeing how she is equally eager with the other man as she is with you, will destroy some of the magic. If she is less eager, she probably is not really enjoying it and will resent you later on.

Believing that such an act is normal and can be done without severe consequences is merely another consequence of porn usage.

People normalize the behavior they witness in porn scenes and believe it is normal to engage in such behaviors themselves. The best these men can do is realize their folly before turning their fantasy into reality.

THE UTILITARIAN VIEW ON PORN

Some of the readers will have read this far and they have come to the joyous conclusion that they do not watch such pornography. They don't watch interracial porn, they don't watch cuckold porn, they don't watch transgender porn. Their porn is limited to the more vanilla categories. They are not being indoctrinated to be passive, they have no interest in transgender pornography, nor in becoming a cuckold. They don't fantasize about these things. If anything, they would prefer to be the bull that humiliates the other men - despite feeling a little awkward with having another man present while they have sex. They believe you can split porn in good porn and bad porn, and they believe watching the right kind of porn can have benefits.

Besides, watching porn is what men do, right? It is perfectly normal for a man with a sex-drive to be watching porn. They know they can not have sex any time they want, so sometimes they need to release their sexual pressure themselves. All men masturbate, and for masturbation you need porn. What other options do these men have? Should they become so desperate for sex that they will engage in sex with women they are not actually attracted to? Women that will pass on diseases? Women that they will be ashamed of having sex with in hindsight? Surely, to avoid such irrational decisions they need to soothe their minds by masturbating. On top of that, the porn these men watch is supposed to make them more dominant. They watch porn to learn new moves and observe new ways of having great sex. They feel convinced that watching a 'facial abuse' video will only increase your manliness. It will help you in exhibiting equally dominant behavior next time you take a girl to bed. Porn, to them, is a way to learn new methods.

Well, they are still wrong. There is no such thing as 'good' porn, there is no such thing as 'harmless' porn consumption, and if they would be honest with themselves, then they would acknowledge that they are not watching it to learn useful tips and tricks. Besides, how many hours of porn consumption are needed for study purposes? They are always watching to feel dopamine flow through their brain and work themselves towards an orgasm, a feeling that they have longed for and are addicted to. Everything else is a poor excuse to justify their behavior and deny the reality.

There is no way around it that sex has a dominant and a submissive partner. Only one party truly controls the rhythm, the position, the initiation, and everything else that is involved. The difference between the dominant role and the submissive, passive role is greater in some couples than in other couples, but it always exists. If you're not sure who is in control, it's probably not you. It is similar to dancing - and here we are talking about ballroom dancing such as the waltz - the man needs to be the one that leads the woman across the dancefloor. He guides her and his movements inform her on what to do and which steps to take. Dancing, nor sex, can have two people that take the lead. A ship never has two captains. When the man is not dominant, it becomes very easy to take on the submissive role instead. It forces the woman to take on the dominant role, a role she may not want and that she fills half heartedly and with a lack of vigor.

What happens when the man starts to feel comfortable in his submissive role? Suddenly the man fantasizes about what a woman will do to him. He fantasizes about experiencing her desire for him. He surrenders to the woman, what he enjoys most is a blowjob and having the woman on top. In those positions the woman can 'do the work' and he can lay back while he feels desired and enjoys her strokes. His least favorite position is taking a girl from behind, since this is the most animalistic, the most dominant position for the man.

The viewer, or the consumer, of porn is rarely dominant when they have sex in real life. This is possible perhaps when a viewer has plenty of sex in real life and watches porn on a rare occasion. Obviously the less porn you watch, the less severe the consequences. Then, when watching porn, they must have a fantasy going of how it is actually them that is having sex with the girl they are watching. Placing yourself in the role of the male that has sex with the woman diminishes any move towards submissiveness. They must be watching a video that makes it relatively easy for them to pretend this is the case. Sometimes, with the right amount of effort, they will succeed. It takes a certain effort to achieve it, and it is easier to fantasize about being the man that has sex with the woman when using your own memories. Nobody that watches porn frequently will be able to watch it from a dominant perspective all the time. Your mind is still clearly registering what you are seeing, which is without a doubt a different man that is penetrating the woman. In the long-term whoever attempts to only watch porn with dominant thoughts will soon find that this is impossible. They will rapidly descent into a passive and submissive attitude. You cannot cheat your way out of the effects of any other addiction, and the same goes for porn.

Men that watch aggressive porn are first and foremost enjoying their arousal, they are not learning how to be dominant but they are giving in to their addiction. They are not on a path to enlightenment. They are wasting their time on a path towards desensitization and restlessness. If they were truly dominant, they would be having sexual intercourse with women, or a single beloved woman, instead of watching some flickering lights on their computer screens while tightly holding their own penis in a grip of death.

So why would people watch this type of pornography? The answer is quite straightforward; they like to watch others suffer. The Germans call it 'schadenfreude', being happy that another is experiencing pain, loss, or an awkward moment. The whole internet is filled with compiled videos of other people failing and hurting themselves. People that are at the bottom of society usually like to see others fall as well. Poor people are envious of the rich, and prefer to hear stories of lottery winnings going to waste, rather than hearing of people that became rich and successful. Misery loves company, and these people prefer to see that they are not alone in their desperate state. Simply put, they prefer to be miserable together with others - hence where the saying 'misery loves company' finds its origin. A porn consumer does not like to see a girl that is happily married or in a healthy relationship, a porn consumer enjoys watching women defile themselves. He enjoys being able to look down on someone else for a change, so that he is distracted from being the pathetic consumer himself.

What bondage, or other more brutal forms of porn, does is that it brings the woman into a submissive state. Think about it, is the viewer connecting to the dominant man (or in some cases the dominant woman), or are they connecting with that weak woman that is being whipped? Even if they don't consciously make this connection to the weaker woman, subconsciously their brain is registering that they are picturing someone experience pain and humiliation, and that this is feeding their arousal. In porn, the protagonist that you connect to is always the woman. The effect you believe such porn has on your brain, may not match with what your brain is subconsciously registering.

Even if you fantasize about being the guy that does it to them, you are not winning this game. You enjoy that fantasy to feel in control, like you have any power. It makes you feel good and break away from reality. After all, the reality is you are alone, and porn has its appeal in that it can offer things you do not experience in real life. Just like video games have its appeal in being able to explore and go on adventures, something you cannot do in real life. After you finish watching, reality comes back and you are powerless once more. Because this fantasy is the only thing that can provide such feelings, it only becomes more addictive. Once you are addicted and return to porn to feel good, you will end up watching it so often that you cannot manage to pretend to be the dominant character all the time.

You lack so much control, that your fantasy and porn use turns into pretending to control someone else. They fantasize about having influence on someone else? The reality is of course that that girl is getting paid and has agreed beforehand to participate in it, you are watching a show. Moreover, it is this show that has control over you. You are consuming it, which is exactly what the producers want. If you are watching actual abuse videos on the darker sides of the web, then you may want to ask yourself what has become of you that you take pleasure, sexual pleasure even, in watching women get abused.

You probably would never perform such behavior in real life, or even want to, so why are you watching it? Simple, the illusion of power combined with complete desensitization. These videos would have never appealed to you, or aroused you, before you descended into more extreme videos. Pretending to have power has always been appealing, but in fact it is the porn that has power over you. All men like power, even Nietzsche wrote about 'the will to power'. You crave this type of porn, because it fills the hole that you are lacking. It fills your inability to exert any power in real life. Nietzsche claimed this was people's driving force in life, but for the porn consumer it does not drive them towards anything other than fueling their addiction and living in a fantasy land.

The inability to fulfil this desire in your life, is exactly what makes it so appealing, so comforting, to connect to the girl in the videos. She is also powerless, but she has learned to enjoy that powerless position. She feels how you feel, but she takes joy and arousal out of it. A part of you may start to desire to transform your misery into that same ecstasy. To copy the behaviors of the person you are watching, and experience the same arousal and euphoria out of it. Instead of making an attempt to change their frustrated, powerless, lives, these men decide to double down on it and fetishize it. And so they start to enjoy their submissive role in life.

PORN AIMED AT WOMEN

Women watch more aggressive, rough, hardcore and gangbang porn, relatively, to men. Overall men may watch a lot more porn than women, but when women do watch porn they are more likely to search for gangbangs and aggressive porn. Why do women view such gangbangs? We know that the more rough, primal form of gangbangs, where the woman is indeed submissive and being used, can be very appealing to women. Let it be clear that this does not mean women are interested in letting just any man have sex with them, but it is the thought of being so strongly desired by all these men. She takes pleasure in imagining pleasing all these men at the same time.

Women love the idea of having multiple men fawn over them. That they unleash in the men this insatiable lust, a lust that only they can aid with. The woman is on the receiving end of this ultimate desire. She gets to experience exactly how much these men want to have her. For women it is thus natural to relate to the submissive woman on video. Even for women that would not at all be comfortable to act out these scenarios in real life, such a fantasy can bring relief. They can relinquish control over their bodies and grant it to these handsome, fit, male performers. For some women, this may make them interested in for example a threesome with two men in real life. Apart from increasing their promiscuity, it does not change their mindset much. Women were submissive from the beginning, and porn does not change that.

These women will of course have no interest in the Bukake style videos where ugly, fat men rub their dicks off in front of their face. No, the gangbang requires a different style of male performer. A performer that looks good enough for the woman to imagine allowing him to ravage her. A woman feels much more valued when a man of higher value shows an interest in her, compared to a man of lower value. A gangbang involving old, ugly, fat men - men generally recognized to have low value and unappealing to women - will not be very arousing to most women. Rather, they will experience disgust. For women, the performers need to be fit, young, handsome men - men that are viewed by all women as attractive partners. When these men are involved, the fantasy for the woman comes to life. The same principle applies in real life, where women value a compliment from a high status male a lot more, compared to a compliment from a low status male. For the low status male, regardless of how well phrased the compliment was, they will feel contempt and disgust. A woman, after all, has to protect her eggs and she needs to mate with genetically strong suitors. Since a man can deposit his sperm in multiple women in a single day, this principle does not apply. Biology still guides our behaviors and social interactions.

Although this rough fantasy may not be shared by all women, it is rather common. It is a natural drive, and women that deny such fantasies are likely still uncomfortable with their bodies or do so for religious or cultural reasons. Nevertheless, it is a fantasy. The core of this fantasy is submission. Submission to a group of strong desirable men, who lose their minds over your body. This ability to make the men go wild with lust, this provides the woman with a certain power. The gangbang fantasy is highly connected to rape fantasy.

Porn sites came up with a way to break the taboo of women watching porn. They created female friendly porn - an ideological version of porn, made to satisfy feminists that believed women were mistreated in porn. Magically, feminists have gone from opposing prostitution and porn, to claiming it is a sign of female liberation. The other porn still exists, but they added a subcategory called female friendly. The genre is a lot more tender, and sensual. More than any other genre it focuses on the woman's pleasure. It highlights how she enjoys what is happening. The porn is designed for women to connect to the performer and picture experiencing what she is experiencing. Now, imagine what happens when men watch these kinds of videos.

Overall porn is made primarily for men. Men consume more in a single session, and consume more frequently. Some women may get addicted to porn as well, and end up masturbating obsessively - reaching a nymphomaniac state of hypersexuality. This can lead to severe consequences as it can translate easily to increased promiscuity. For women, almost any woman can become promiscuous. There will always be a man willing to have sex with her. For men, this is a lot more difficult. This means that hypersexualized women that are addicted to porn can more easily live their fantasies - resulting in a higher chance of sexually transmitted diseases and unplanned pregnancy. It may also increase the woman's insecurities as she compares her body and sexual performance to that of a pornstar. No gender is safe from the effects of pornography on the human mind.

*''Every single time a man sleeps with a lot of women, he's called a stud. But if a woman sleeps with a lot of men, she's called a slut, and people think this is unfair... Nah. It's completely fair, and I'll tell you why, alright? Because it's ****ing easy to be a slut. It's ****ing hard to be a stud. To be a stud you have to be witty, charming, be well-dressed, have nice shoes, and a fake job. To be a slut you just have to be there. There are fat ugly sluts out there. There are not fat ugly studs.''*

- Jim Jefferies, Comedian

THE GREATEST SUFFERING

Does porn hurt men the most? No. Porn hurts women more, and in more 'real' ways than it hurts men. We do not want to depict men as the gender that is losing out due to porn, we sincerely believe all people involved lose. Porn is a game without any winners. Everyone that plays loses, and everyone that knows someone that plays the game will lose as well. A worse game is hardly imaginable, although Russian roulette comes to mind as a close match.

Both men and women suffer, but it should be clear from the title of this book alone that our focus is on how it affects men. In male culture, porn is considered to be something normal. Those that refrain from watching porn risk ridicule and are not understood by their peers. When all the world has gone crazy, it is those that are sane that are labelled as the most crazy of all.

''A time will come when the whole world will go mad. And to anyone who is not mad they will say: 'You are mad, for you are not like us.''

- St. Anthony the Great

Men are ignorant of the effects of porn on themselves and on society. They fail to recognize the harm it does to them. Porn is introduced to young boys, as a harmless way to pass time. It is introduced as a sign of maturing. Grown ups watch it, and if you are a young boy this is your rite of passage into adulthood. Or, so many believe at least.

The reason that this chapter is not at the start of the book, is to make clear that our main concern is men. A lot of men dismiss most arguments against watching this poison on their mind as being feminist ramblings. They will fight back, stating that their favorite porn 'stars' are doing it voluntarily and earning good money. They love their job, or so they believe, and that makes watching porn absolutely moral. In other cases, the men have simply reached levels of misogyny that they no longer care about the welfare of the women that they are watching. Whatever you believe, there are other reasons, as shown in this book, to stop watching porn.

The argument I make is not a moral argument. It is, to phrase Nietzsche again, beyond good and evil. We are not concerned with the question if porn is morally justifiable or not. Although, it would be hard to draft a moral framework where the porn industry is morally justifiable - it can only exist in a world that has surpassed morals. We are concerned with the question of what porn does to you and your masculinity, your virility. But before we go back to that, we cannot write a book about the adverse effects of pornography, without addressing the elephant in the room.

Do women in porn suffer? Pornography is in its essence equal to paying a prostitute extra in order to be allowed to record her on video. At least, for the voluntary porn - which most men believe is the only type of porn. Many men refuse to believe that not all women are there by voluntary choices. Some women are intimidated or threatened to perform in a pornographic movie. The quote below belongs to Linda Boreman, who featured in movies in the 1970's. She is better known under her nickname Linda Lovelace, and she acquired fame by starring in the classic porn movie 'Deep Throat'. A movie that allowed porn to enter into mainstream consumption.

"My initiation...was a gang rape by five men... It was the turning point in my life. He threatened to shoot me with the pistol if I didn't go through with it. I had never experienced anal sex before and it ripped me apart. They treated me like an inflatable plastic doll, picking me up and moving me here and there. They spread my legs this way and that, shoving their things at me and into me, they were playing musical chairs with parts of my body. I have never been so frightened and disgraced and humiliated in my life. I felt like garbage. I engaged in sex acts for pornography against my will, to avoid being killed. The lives of my family were threatened."

- Linda Boreman

It is beyond all doubt that this was a horrible, traumatic experience for her. She is not the only one that entered the industry by this method - yet men still masturbate to her videos when they find them online, ignorant to the circumstances around it.

There is also the 'revenge' porn where women made a video with their boyfriend or husband and the man places it online after breaking up with the woman, or more likely, after getting dumped by the woman. You may consider the women naive and too trustworthy, but this is human nature. Trust is a fundamental part of any relationship, and most couples don't plan for it to end. It is a cruel method of getting revenge; to broadcast their naked body onto the internet for eternity. In many countries this has been criminalized, but it may be difficult to catch the perpetrators, or for the women to even discover the man has been sharing her photos online.

There is also the unwitting porn, where women are too drunk to notice, or the camera is placed in a hidden location, and the women are simply not aware of being recorded. The widespread hook-up culture has made this fairly easy when the man brings a woman back to his room and has a camera set up somewhere in a corner of the room. Although they may get drunk themselves, some women are drugged and completely unaware of what has happened to them. These are of course less common, and a tiny niche compared to all the porn available on the internet, but that does mean it still happens. The quote below is taken from court documents in the case against Lavont Flanders and Emerson Callum, who were convicted for drugging, raping and videotaping women over several years.

"Some of the victims do not remember anything until the following day, when they awoke, half-naked and semiconscious, either in their own cars or in their hotel rooms, sometimes covered in vomit or urine."

The men are spending life behind bars. Gemase Lee Simmons would pose as a modelling agency, and required girls to let him take nude, and sexually explicit photographs. He claimed this was necessary for them to get recruited, but in reality he used these pictures to blackmail them into further sexual acts. Some of his victims were minors. He is spending his time in prison. Both of these groups of women are unwilling participants in the grander scheme of what is online pornography.

There are, however, countless women that are more than

happy to participate in the creation of this material. For a small fee, of course. It is somewhat remarkable how cheap it is to convince a woman to take her clothes off on video and be naked for eternity for the entire world to see. The women are attracted by fame and a lack of foresight. Again, only in an amoral society could people desire the type of fame that pornography brings. It would appear that, funny as it may sound, porn has normalized porn. We consume so much porn as a society and porn has become so acceptable to watch, that women no longer see shame in participating in the creation of it. It has become a normal part of our society.

"There is no justification for the amount of naked people on the World Wide Web, many of whom are clearly (clearly!) doing so for non-monetary reasons. Where were these people fifteen years ago? Were there really millions of women in 1986 turning to their husbands and saying, 'You know, I would love to have total strangers masturbate to images of me deep-throating a titanium dildo, but there's simply no medium for that kind of entertainment. I guess we'll just have to sit here and watch Falcon Crest again.'" - Chuck Klosterman

Considering the lifelong impact of someone at your work, or a future partner, discovering the material. Or, imagine, family members, or parents, stumbling upon it. It is hardly a surprise that many performers have left their old lives behind and have a poor relationship with their family and friends. Likely, for many of them, these bonds were not that strong to begin with. You could argue that it would almost be more decent to be a prostitute, especially when thinking of highly paid top quality escorts. Prostitutes know discretion, and can keep their source of income a secret. These women earn more for a single night of discrete pleasure, than do our porn models for a lifelong presence on the sex-side of the web.

Some women, assumably, are too gullible and believe the men when they say the material will not be shown online, but only in a store on the other side of the world. Many will lack the foresight to realize the consequences of their actions, and are drawn in by making some quick money for what is ultimately easy work. It should not surprise anyone that there are plenty of people on the world that are bad at making decisions.

The vast majority of those that perform in porn do so for only one, or a few videos. A decent mid-section of the group will make dozens of videos before quitting or being discarded. Very few, a tiny minority, become the famous models that make hundreds upon hundreds of videos. Plenty of women that enter the industry will try to reach that height of fame though, and they are willing to make sacrifices for it.

.

"Like most porn performers, I perpetuated this lie. One of my favorite things to say when asked if I liked doing a particular scene was, 'I only do what I like! I wouldn't do it if I didn't like it!' I would say this with a big fake smile and giggle. What a total lie! I did what I had to do to get work in porn. I did what I knew would help me gain fame in the industry."

- Vanessa Belmond

142

The majority will have to go through the rest of their life working in a regular job, with this anvil always hanging over their head. The constant dread of hoping nobody will discover their video online, that nobody will recognize them. And yet these are the girls that got lucky, they got out early, before things got worse. Perhaps lucky isn't the best term, but at least they are alive. Even a single abusive video online for all of the ages will severely diminish the satisfaction they can get in the rest of their lives. Read another quote from a supposedly empowered, liberated woman.

"It was the most degrading, embarrassing, horrible thing ever. I had to shoot an interactive DVD, which takes hours and hours of shooting time, with a 104 degree fever! I was crying and wanted to leave but my agent wouldn't let me, he said he couldn't let me flake on it. I also did a scene where I was put with male talent that was on my 'no list'. I wanted to please them so I did it. He stepped on my head [...] I freaked out and started bawling; they stopped filming and sent me home with reduced pay since they got some shot but not the whole scene."

- Jessi

It is to hope that they don't end up committing suicide over it, but they would not be the first to do so. Most likely, if you have watched videos over a period of a few years, some of the women you watched have killed themselves and might have been dead already when you were viewing her video.

For whatever reason women get into porn, once they are in, it may be difficult to get out. At least as long as you are desired, once that passes you get kicked out with no benefits or retirement plan and you have to scramble to find a new job. Possibly you have to move back in with family, or possibly they still had a primary job while shooting the scenes on the side. While the porn producers want you to work for them, they will intimidate you and bully you into signing a contract that vaguely states you have to do whatever they tell you. Let's imagine what happens to a woman that is desired and stays in the business.

She will be pushed more and more, further and further away from her comfort zone. From vanilla, regular, sex, she slowly degrades into the more humiliating porn that everyone seems to adore. From receiving missionary position sex, to having a group of men run a train on you isn't always an easy step. The women are bullied into more extreme kinds of porn, especially if they want to keep their 'career' going. They will be reluctant, but simultaneously desperate. Surrounded by a large group of men, alone, far away from their friends and family, these young girls do not feel like they have much of a choice. With small incremental steps they will be pushed into doing more and more on camera. Like a frog that stays in the bowl if it's slowly boiling water, only to end up boiled to death, so the porn performer stays in the industry while the porn gets increasingly degrading, only to end up overdosed on drugs.

Not to mention the prevalence of STDs and other illnesses and destructions on the body. Frequent testing of HIV may prevent that spreading into their group of core actors, but other diseases are frequently spread. Still HIV has called plenty of performers in the past, and it is one of the reasons some women refuse to work with men that also perform in gay scenes. All sorts of bacteria and viruses like herpes and HPV are accepted as a part of the job. Their anus will never be the same after inserting the ginormous objects that some place inside to stretch their sphincter. The anal prolapse occurs when the inner part of the rectum falls out of their butthole and the pink flesh is visible outside. It is disgusting, but these 'rosebuds' as they are called are more popular in porn than ever. Before they would be hidden from camera, now they are the highlight of a scene and get a close-up to share with the viewer. Such anal prolapses can leave lasting consequences to their bowel system, and they might require rectal surgery to tie things back together. It is a sacrifice they are pushed into by the porn producers that want to make more extreme material that is not wildly available for free yet, and an ever growing extreme taste in the global audience. Their bodies will take a toll on what they are put through, but the mental toll won't be any less.

What does it do to a woman that has sex with over a hundred, or a thousand, men on camera? The most extraordinary sexual positions are tried on her, her body gets pushed to its limits. What kind of life is possible after that? What kind of man would want to settle down with a woman like that? Frankly, plenty of men will want to settle down with her - but these are either creepy admirers or men from within the porn industry. How will she be able to adjust to a regular life?

Should it be any surprise that drug use among this group is common, as a way to cope with the extreme circumstances of their existence. In a way, you may argue that these women are ruined. At least ruined for a normal existence inside a normal relationship. Some of them manage to cope better than others, but the presence of an exception to the rule does not disprove the rule. Even the women that give interviews and pretend to be happy with their role, they will have to say so to sway their audience and can not share the truth. Most men would not want to watch porn, knowing that they are watching a suicidal woman. Everything a performer says, it is all part of the act. It is all a part of enticing you. These women are aware that by creating a following of fans, they can increase their income. Besides, they love the appreciation, the attention, and the fame. And in the amoral world they live in, what else would they pursue besides money?

145

We assume it is fair to say, that the women are not happy in their job, that there is no other option than to conclude women in porn are suffering. Perhaps some may be content with their life, or claim to be, but that does not apply to the group as a whole. Nonetheless, let's provide some more stories in order to make this argument more convincing.

The quotes below are from pornstars that share the reality of their daily life. It is a life of drug and alcohol abuse, paid for by their porn income. The drug and alcohol usage can only relieve their feelings of depression momentarily, after which it hits back twice as hard. It is, as everyone knows, not a long-term solution to these problems.

"After a year or so of that so-called 'glamorous life,' I sadly discovered that drugs and drinking were part of the lifestyle. I began to drink and party of out control—cocaine, alcohol, and ecstasy were my favorites. Before long, I turned into a person I did not want to be. After doing so many hardcore scenes, I couldn't do it anymore. I just remember being in horrible situations and experiencing extreme depression and being alone and sad."

- Andi

"People in the porn industry are numb to real life and are like zombies walking around. The abuse that goes on in this industry is completely ridiculous. The way

these young ladies are treated is totally sick and brainwashing. I left due to the trauma I experienced even though I was there only a short time. I hung out with a lot of people in the adult industry, everybody from contract girls to gonzo actresses. Everybody has the same problems. Everybody is on drugs. It's an empty lifestyle trying to full up a void. I became horribly addicted to heroin and crack. I overdosed at least three times, had tricks pull knives on me, have been beaten half to death..."

- Jessie

"It was torture for seven years. I was miserable, I was lonely, I eventually turned to drugs and alcohol and attempted suicide. I knew I wanted out, but I didn't know how to get out."

- Brittni Ruiz

Are these women really so depressed and miserable? Let's share a few examples of women that ended up taking their own lives. Normally, it is very rare for women to commit suicide, but it seems a lot more common inside the world of pornography.

On December the 15th, 2017, Yuri Luv was found dead in her apartment. She was discovered by her landlord. She was 31. It is believed she overdosed on pills.

On January the 19th, 2018, Olivia Lua died while in rehab. She was 23. She was in rehab for a prescription drug addiction. There may be a connection between being a porn performer and having a prescription drug addiction, or so you could think.

On January 10th, 2018, the 20-year-old Olivia Nova passed away. Her agent confirmed the news and was kind enough to say it was a "beautiful girl" and that she had a "gentle personality". What could have killed a gentle girl like this? Her real name was Lexi Forde and she was discovered in her bed, naked from the waist down with bruises on her leg. The autopsy indicated she had died from sepsis brought on by a urinary tract infection that had spread to her kidneys. Additionally, Lexi had a drinking problem and had been warned her days could be numbered if she did not turn sober.

On November 9th, 2017, Amanda Friedland, also known as Shyla Stylez, was found dead while staying at her mother's home.

On December 5th, 2017, Mercedes Gabrowski killed herself. She was better known as August Ames. She had rejected a scene with an actor that also performed in homosexual scenes, and was called homophobic. The reason she rejected the scene was concerns about her safety, and to avoid STDs. She was known to already suffer from long-term depression and decided to end the controversy by ending her own life. She was married, but her husband was a director in the porn industry.

This was a group that died together in the same brief time span, but we can go further back.

On January 28th, 2005, Karen Lancaume overdosed on temazepam and alcohol. She had been gradually gotten addicted to drugs and alcohol after her career took off with a boom.

In March 1984, Shauna Grant shot herself in the head. She had turned into a drug addict after shooting over thirty movies.

On December 29, 2002, Vivien Neves committed suicide. She had been the first nude model in The Times and was a well-known performer back then.

On July 19th, 2008, Anastasia Blue committed suicide by taking an overdose of Tylenol. She had been suffering from depression since her career in porn.

On September 17th, 2000, Paula Yates committed suicide by taking an overdose of heroine. Or, alternatively, she accidentally overdosed. In any case, she had a heroin addiction.

On July 31st, 2002, Pauline Chan committed suicide by jumping off a building. She had been in the hospital numerous times due to her drug abuse habits. She also suffered depression.

On March 12th, 2009, Leila Lopes committed suicide by taking a drug overdose.

On December 19th, 2010, Violet Adamson committed suicide by hanging herself. She was 35, and had filmed her first hardcore scene three years before.

On June 16th, 1990, Megan Leigh shot herself in the head. On top of that, she had taken an overdose of Valium that to a normal person would have been a lethal dose on its own.

In 1995 Alex Jordan hanged herself at the age of 31. She had appeared in over 166 pornographic movies.

A few more... Haley Paige in 2005, drugs. Savannah, shot herself, 1995. Chloe Jones died in 2005 after liver failure, caused by long-term alcohol abuse. Eva Lux died from a heroin overdose in 2005. Karen Dior died from cirrhosis of the liver and AIDS. Camilla de Castro leaped off a building, towards her death. Angela Devi committed suicide in 2006 by asphyxiation. Susan Britton killed herself. Juliet Jett died of a heroin overdose in 2005. Rebecca

Steele died from a drug overdose in 2004, it didn't help that she also had AIDS. Celia Young killed herself in 1992. Arcadia Lake died of a drug overdose in 1990. Linda Wong died from a drug and alcohol overdose in 1987. Bambi Woods died of a drug overdose in 1986. Lisa de Leeuw died of AIDS in 1993. In 2002, Elisa Bridges died of heroin overdose. In 2007, Lori Michaels died from a heart defect, likely caused by drugs. Bodil Joensen died from alcohol-induced liver cirrhosis. Sophie Roche killed herself in 2002. Naughtia Childs leaped to her death from a building, in 2002. Jill Munroe died of a heroin overdose in 1982. Tolly Crystal leaped towards her death in 2002. Clarissa Doll killed herself in 2006. Teri Diver overdosed on prescription drugs in 2001. Chanel Price died from a drug overdose in 1992. Kristine Heller killed herself in 1989. Nancee Kellee hanged herself in 1991. Tina Russell died from cirrhosis of the liver due to severe alcohol abuse. Lisa Mendelez died of AIDS in 1999. Wendy O'Williams shot herself. Talia James killed herself. Mary Millington killed herself. In 1998, Trinity died from a drug overdose. In 2008, Missy overdosed on prescription drugs. This list could go on and on. And results are similar for male performers, who also die frequently from excessive drug use and suicide.

Sometimes a single scene can be enough to trigger a suicide. Alyssa Funke starred in a casting couch video, which was soon discovered by her classmates. Her tweets celebrated her "pornstar status", but several days later she grabbed a gun and shot herself.

And what do they have in common? We see a lot of suicide. But we also see a lot of problems with drug and alcohol use. The women are fleeing reality into their own fantasy world. Drugs aren't cheap, so they are pulled into doing more work to earn more money to buy more drugs. The situation may be better for a few women that have their independent agencies, but most women are employed by large firms. Of course, the women that are still working in the industry will never publicly talk about this - it would be the end of their career and source of income.

"Of course I lied to my fans. I led them to believe I lived a fantasy life which was far from the truth. I fed into their fantasies. I said I wanted sex 24/7 and made it seem like I absolutely loved what I did and was living this happy life. I gave them hope and insight into their relationships by telling them what to do. I started to feel like an important nobody, they knew Elizabeth [the porn star], but they would never care to know Jan [the real me]. I had to do whatever the producer pleased and I had to accept it or else no pay. Sometimes you would get to a gig and the producer would change what the scene was supposed to be to something more intense and again if you didn't like it, too bad, you did it or no pay."

- Jan Meza

It must be clear that the women in porn are not to be envied. They are not 'stars', a term this book has tried to avoid, because it is so highly inaccurate, and their lives are not glamorous. The media and the porn industry work together to recognize these women as 'stars'. It is a strong play on rhetoric to make it appear as if pornstars are simply the alternative to being a Hollywood star. They are framed as being equals, in the same league, as both of them are all about fame. This terminology, calling the girls 'stars' is what draws in a lot of new girls. Who doesn't want to become a star? There are even awards for best pornstars. They have millions of followers on Twitter, feeding into their narcissism. It is all part of a big ploy to make porn more appealing to the women.

In reality, they are glorified prostitutes that are slightly better at acting. Or perhaps just more suitable for the camera. Any woman working as a prostitute will say that it is empowering, and liberating. These are buzzwords, introduced by staunch feminists, to justify their behavior. They are uttered to prevent cognitive dissonance. How could they say the work is miserable, when the next day they will be recorded again. Be aware of this misery when you watch porn again, stop fooling yourself into believing all these women really want to be there in that role. But the misery of womankind does not end there. The effects are far more extensive. It is not only the women involved in porn, but women around the world. As every man is familiar with porn, every woman has a man that thinks porn is normal. Almost all, anyway. The men that oppose porn are a tiny minority. What pressures does this place on the woman?

Sexually there are the more intense demands. A girl must give blowjobs like a pornstar, refusing to do so makes her a prude. A girl must be open to receiving anal sex, even when it hurts her more than it gives her pleasure, she will give in to the relentless requests from her partner. She is pushed into buying sexy lingerie, but not only for the bedroom. More revealing clothing becomes normal. Women show off a lot more flesh in daily life than before. With pornstars as the, supposedly, ideal type of women that men dream about, women think they should mimic such behavior to get male attention. How else would they compete? So they show off their cleavage, and all of their bodies. Not only in real life, no, they start putting pictures of themselves online. Their success in life is measured by getting more men to drool over them and give their photos 'likes'. It is a combination of the effects of the internet and social networking and a culture of porn. Nevertheless, we could say this is their personal choice. It is not purely due to porn, but a wider societal change where people are isolated, atomized and shouting for attention.

They also suffer from a lack of competent men. Porn has

created the largest shortage of eligible men since World War One wiped out millions and pushed them face-first into the muddy fields of Flanders. It was this absence of men that created the first wave of feminism and demands for voting rights for women. Modern men may not be physically dead, but mentally they are not far off. They are weak, passive and effeminate. They spend their time on videogames and porn, instead of chasing their dreams and ambitions. Their virility is missing. They do not develop themselves, but distract themselves instead. Such forms of escapism may not be bad when pursued occasionally, but we are witnessing this on a societal level.

Some men go as far as forming the MGTOW movement, or Men Going Their Own Way. Well, who's way would you otherwise go? The term is a euphemism for men that redirect their attention towards porn and video games, that is their own way apparently. Men inside the movement will claim it is about avoiding marriage and the legal trappings that come with it, but it does not appear that they show true virility in their actions. Fleeing into a fantasy world of video games, and fueling their porn addiction. Some men that embrace the term do focus on career, or on hooking up frequently with different women. They are expected to eventually get bored of taking home a drunk girl from a club and grow out of their phase. Many men that embrace the term are in fact disgruntled divorced men, whose wives have taken half their belongings and who they have to pay a large monthly figure in alimony.

Modern society has succeeded in antagonizing men and women, as if they are enemies. Men versus women. Somehow the idea has risen up that men and women cannot both win, which is utterly ridiculous. Men and women need one another to live happy and satisfied lives. One cannot reach contentment without the involvement of the other. It is the full equality of the sexes, an egalitarian approach even, an unnatural idea in itself, that has been the origin of the idea that men and women compete for the same goals. The lack of cooperation and differentiation is a direct cause of the low fertility rates in nearly every part of the world except for Africa.

This nonsensical equality of the sexes is only possible due to the lack of manliness in our young men. Men need to reclaim their natural position in the world, the role of leader. The one that carries responsibility, and receives admiration for it. All of this hiding into a world of online obscenities is a hiding from responsibility. Embrace the tasks that give you satisfaction, that allow you to accomplish something in this life, accomplish anything. The Greeks called it eudaimonia, a feeling of lasting bliss, satisfaction and contentment. Modern men chase mere pleasure, they are hedonists in the purest sense of the word. Hedonists chase pleasure at every moment of the day, one distraction from their dreadful existence is followed immediately by another.

Porn makes them feel happy, so they watch porn. Video games make them feel happy, so they play video games. Drinking alcohol makes them happy, so they get drunk on the weekends. Weed makes them feel happy, so they smoke weed before sleeping. Yes, all these things make you feel happy, while you are doing them. Once you stop, you are faced with the reality of your life again. You are faced with being an incompetent loser that is not accomplishing all that you can accomplish. There are so many missed opportunities, so many chances to get more out of your life. You are not making an impact on the people or the world around you. Your existence is equal to that of a beast, you exist for the sake of existing. You are led blindly by following your deepest instincts, the ancient instincts that are easily fooled in the modern world. Perhaps you would like a simpler life, that of a beast. Perhaps you believe that your life would be easier as a woman, that women are offered everything they could want on a silver platter, and you fantasize about becoming a woman. Unfortunately for you, you are born as a man, and you will have to be a man. Yet, is it really unfortunate that you are born as a man? You should realize how many opportunities life has presented you with, as a man you can make your life great if you make the right decisions and take responsibility over your life. Face life head-on and grab the bull by the horns, instead of acting like Peter Pan and never growing up into adulthood. Peter Pan was a book written for children, children that were afraid of the future and enjoyed fantastical stories. It was not a manual on how to live a good life. It may not be the easiest life, compared to that of a housecat that lays around and eats, but it is a more rewarding life. At least, it can be a more rewarding life. The fulfillment of this life is up to the individual.

When men take care of themselves, their bodies and their mind, women will flow towards these men. They will admire you and look up to you. The 'desire' that men feel they are missing, this desire comes in the form of admiration. Yet instead of taking up responsibility and gathering this admiration, they want to take the 'easy' way out and envy the desire women receive for their bodies. Instead of acquiring this desire by sake of their virtue, they want to copy women and also receive admiration over their bodies.

If only men were to make that shift, how great it would be for all the women in the world. There would once more be a superfluous amount of eligible men that could captivate them. Men that they could rely on and surrender to. Once more there would be men that make them desire to be a mother, men whose genes they would be happy to pass on and merge with their own. No longer would they need to go out clubbing, to battle over the most appealing men that go to such places. Only to sleep with this man as a sign of their high status and some fleeting fun. The genders could join efforts and make the world a more satisfactory place. A simpler place, with less frustration and conflict. Above all, less depression. Depression is perhaps the greatest disease of our time, but really depression is just losing a purpose in life. Once reinvigorated, the purpose returns, and depression vanishes. With purpose, comes hope, and with hope, come children. Porn only brings depression and despair.

WITH PORN COMES MASTURBATION

It is difficult to talk about porn for so long without talking about masturbation. These usually go together, for although looking at porn can be addicting on its own, it is usually worsened by the combination of masturbation. Masturbation will be followed by orgasm, although that may take a while as men try to postpone their orgasm while watching porn to find the perfect moment. These men perform what is called 'edging', they remain on the edge of orgasm for extended periods of time. This keeps them in a highly aroused state, which they maintain by switching to new videos, bringing novelty and surprise each time. Every video needs to be better, more extreme, than the previous, to keep their attention up. Due to this, a browsing session can take anywhere from a five-minute straight to the point release, all the way to an hours-long binge-consumption of a downward spiral of sexy videos.

Research shows us that porn-users respond more strongly in their arousal by viewing pornographic material than those that do not frequently use porn. This means that the more porn we watch, the more our brains are adjusted to get aroused by it. Masturbation and porn are linked together in the brain, and the brains are adjusted to that. Your brain establishes a new normal. They know that when seeing porn images, an orgasm will follow, so blood starts flowing towards the penis to prepare for this. A man that will not watch porn frequently will feel this arousal upon having an actual woman in his bed, rather than going crazy when seeing the pixels on a screen.

"Consuming pornography does not lead to more sex, it leads to more porn. Much like *eating McDonald's every day will accustom you to food that (although enjoyable) is essentially not food, pornography conditions the consumer to being satisfied with an impression of extreme sex rather than the real." - Virginie Despentes*

A lot of masturbating men believe that this will get them in the right mindset for sex. Yet, it has nothing to do with real sex. They are completely different entities. Porn is masturbation, it is the opposite of sex. The more porn you watch, the more difficult real sex will be.

"Pornography does not promote sex, if one defines sex as a shared act between two partners. It promotes masturbation. It promotes the solitary auto-arousal that precludes intimacy and love. Pornography is about getting yourself off at someone else's expense." - Chris Hedges

The dopamine and oxytocin release from the orgasm is linked by the brain to the porn it is watching, instead of to a real woman. Men lose the ability to bond to a woman when they consume porn, because their brain is trying to bond them to the women on the screen. Love, frankly, is that simple. It is about this oxytocin hormone that is released. The more you have sex with someone, the more bonding hormones, called oxytocin, are released and the more you care for them. You can welcome oxytocin in a relationship, as it is the cornerstone of every happy marriage. Yet what benefit does it serve when it is bonding your brain to some porn actress? In a relationship, the effect serves the purpose of the couple staying together, at least for the period of infancy of the child. This is why the initial oxytocin rush usually slows after a year to a year-and-a-half and that is when a lot of people 'fall out of love' and break up. Nothing changed for these couples, other than their oxytocin levels. Though that process of oxytocin release can be repeated indefinitely, of course. For successful couples the oxytocin keeps being shared with every orgasm they have, but lower doses are also released for smaller activities like holding hands. As long as physical contact is involved.

It should then be no surprise that porn leads to divorce, as men lose the level of generosity towards their wives that they had before. This generosity is now directed towards a multitude of women on screen. Some men, that watch the same woman over and over again, may even fall in love with the porn model. A fully natural and logical reaction from the brain, only foolish to act upon. It is foolish to continue to trick your brain into believing this. These men believe that what they experience is true love, and become infatuated with this woman. Infatuation means seeing someone as flawless, divine or godlike even. It comes closer to worship, than to respect. Love is the natural result of oxytocin, making us more generous and caring towards a person, but not ignoring their flaws. Being in love is closer to infatuation, or a more passionate form of love that emphasizes lust. Hence at the start of a relationship people are more likely to overlook the other's flaws. There are other reasons why porn leads to divorce, obviously, as the wives feel neglected, insecure and offended by their husband's preference for porn instead of them. Nobody is happy to be in a relationship with an addict - whether its drugs, alcohol, or porn does not matter much.

Some believe that a man should ejaculate at least once a week to keep the sperm young and healthy. They also think that this provides the greatest peak in testosterone, which takes place around a week since the last ejaculation. Testosterone does peak after a week, but shortly after ejaculation it drops. Is it better to have a level that swings up and down, or one that remains equal at an elevated level? It is doubtful to say the least that in the long-run masturbation is beneficial for your testosterone. More likely your average level of testosterone will be reduced by your frequent masturbation.

Why do you even care about testosterone? It is probably because you are concerned about being a real man. A masculine man. A man with virility. A man that can attract women. A man that is not seen as a wimp by others. Well, if you care about this it will be more effective to go and pick up weights in the gym, than to sit in your dark room watching filth. Women are not aroused by men that masturbate to some porn, it won't make you more manly or attractive in their eyes. Besides picking up weights, you can find other methods to increase your testosterone. In the worst case, you can visit a doctor and they may be able to help you out with your low testosterone levels. Low testosterone can be a real health risk, and it can heighten your exposure to feelings of depression, so it is a good topic to care about. Still, you are lying to yourself if you say you have to masturbate to keep those levels elevated - you will succeed in achieving the exact opposite, your testosterone long-term average will drop.

Perhaps it is better to have young sperm, but that only matters when you are trying to conceive a child. If you are trying to conceive a child, you would not need to be masturbating anyway. You would try to release every load you have into your woman to increase the chances of a sperm finding the egg. If you are trying to get your wife or girlfriend, or whomever, pregnant, it would not help to have a reduced amount of sperm that you are ejaculating, due to emptying your sack the day before on some online videos. No, you would be savoring your precious soldiers and sending all of them into the battlefield. You would not be at risk of having 'old' sperm. More likely, your body will be exhausted from constantly producing new sperm.

Lastly, there are those that say frequent orgasms, say once a week, are good for men to prevent certain type of cancers. Research on it is not conclusive, so let's not overestimate the health benefit there. Still, we can imagine that in the future there will be better evidence and it will say that having an orgasm once a week does reduce your risk for some cancers. Primarily prostate cancer. Does that mean porn is good for you? No, you could reach that once a week by either having normal sexual intercourse, or masturbating without the use of porn.

We must conclude that these ideas of masturbation being good for these reasons, are lies and make-believe that men use to justify their addiction. It is not a choice, it is not a rational decision to think it is time to unleash some sperm to keep the production going. It is an ad hoc justification of what just took place. A way to avoid feeling the guilt of your lack of self control. Most of all, even if there were a positive reason for masturbation, it would not require porn to be effective.

What about the nature of male sexuality? Men believe they have these insatiable urges to masturbate. They cannot focus on any other task, it is too distracting. While they are in this horny, aroused, state they figure it must be better to watch some porn and feel like their normal selves again afterwards. They should ask themselves, is it truly the release of sperm that you crave, or did your mind wander and started to fantasize about the many thrilling movies that are only a click away. Are you craving to masturbate, or craving to indulge into your addiction. How could you even tell the difference, since both have the same origin.

Consider masturbating without porn. If your desire is truly to masturbate, then this should satisfy your urge. Men lived an eternity without porn, so let's not pretend that this is a shocking proposal. It proposes to go back in time around ten or twenty years, before free high-speed online porn was available everywhere. If you are horny, you should not need any additional stimulants to bring yourself to orgasm. Perhaps you will fantasize about a girl you saw, or a past sexual experience, to quicken the result. Do not look at pictures, or any sort of soft porn or solovideos. See how much you enjoy this experience.

It will be a rather unsatisfying experience. It was not the release that you desired, it did not give you the same high, it did not bring you to the same levels of arousal. It will be a disappointment, since it did not feed into your addiction. Cease your porn consumption, and see how often you truly wish to masturbate. It will feel so empty, but perhaps sometimes you need this in order to be able to focus. Despite this orgasm not giving you the same high, it will allow you to regain your focus. This is opposed to the result of masturbating to porn, which will only make you more aroused.

When you watch porn to lower your level of arousal, you will surely fail. You will watch a few videos and become only more aroused. Your mind goes into its state of recognizing the superfluous amount of fertile women in your surroundings, and kick its arousal into overdrive. Even after you orgasm, the memory of the multitude of wombs to be impregnated lives on in your brain. Within a brief timespan, your brain starts to hint you are ready for the next round. Watching porn to clear your mind of sex, is like the old adage of fighting for peace, fucking for virginity, and drinking alcohol to get sober. Watching sex to stop thinking about sex, who could ever have imagined that this was a bad idea?

Forget all and any rational explanation for your love of porn, your brain is bonded to the porn sites and you have an addiction. Whether it is mild or severe does not matter, porn creates addicts the first second they view it. It is so tempting, but none of it is real and all of our minds are tricked. Procreation is our strongest natural desire and all men are easily fooled by a synthetic version of it. Nevertheless, even an eternity of porn can not bring about the tiniest piece of eudaimonia. Like the Tantalus-torture, porn will never bring satisfaction.

HYPERSEXUAL AND HOMOSEXUAL

In this chapter, we will attempt to explain what hypersexuality is by a comparison to the homosexual community. Large parts of the homosexual community are highly hypersexual. We will not make the hypothesis that homosexuality has its origin in excessive porn use, at least not in a great majority of cases. Some homosexual behaviors that are exhibited in heterosexual men are possibly caused by porn, but actual homosexual tendencies will have other origins and are often apparent long before a child has consumed any porn. Artificial intelligence has already been able to identify which men are gay out of a sample of pictures of men, based on how these men look and what facial structure they have. This clearly confirms the evidence that people are simply born gay. This does not mean that excessive porn use cannot push straight men into homosexual behaviors. Such heterosexual men are usually not attracted to the male physique, but to submissiveness and the penis. Autogynephilia can cause these men to be attracted first of all to their own body and their own penis. This admiration for the penis can then spread to those of other men. Such men may fantasize about another penis, but will not fantasize about kissing a bearded man.

But what exactly is hypersexuality? Hypersexuality is sometimes referred to as compulsive sexual behavior or sexual addiction. It occurs when people spend a large amount of time fantasizing about sex, or use sex as a way to cope with life and to feel better. For gay men this is wildly common, simply go to a nightclub and find someone to get it on with. A similar trend has been on the rise in heterosexual nightclubs. Simply make the night a bit more fun with casual sex with a stranger. It is a temporary distraction on the meaninglessness of their lives. It makes people treat sex in the same way as other addictive substances. If you are feeling down, simply have some sex to feel a bit better.

In the last several decades gays no longer needed to hide underground. The tolerant Western world entered an era of atheism. What constitutes a sin was no longer relevant, and the opinion of the bible on sodomy was deemed intolerant. Tolerance, the last respected virtue of the Western world, allowed the homosexuals to come out of the proverbial closet. It is this same tolerance that allowed massive porn consumption, prostitution, transgenderism, and other vices to proliferate. Tolerance gets mentioned here, as it became a buzzword first when it was used to build acceptance towards the gay world. Later on, the word was embraced to accept immigrants, other religions, and a varying degree of genders. This is not to say that tolerance is bad, but it is abused to open the gates for destructive tools like porn.

Although the Western world likes to imagine that tolerance is a great virtue that is newly discovered, it is as old as time. When people settled in cities and empires were built, rulers needed tolerance towards other religions and customs to prevent civil war. Tolerance has always been applied by rulers to keep their empire from collapse. What is new, perhaps, is that never before has tolerance been the only virtue that is deemed important. To be virtuous has become synonymous to being tolerant. Nonetheless, it is difficult to judge whether we should call that progress. This book is very intolerant towards the porn industry. Of course, some tolerance is always preferable to no tolerance, as can be witnessed in countries around the world where homosexuals are hacked to pieces or hanged.

In this tolerant, de-Christianized world, the homosexual community appeared on the surface of society. Not celebrating homosexuality is now considered intolerant. This allows hypersexuality to take place in public as nobody dares to say anything negative about it. Everyone is afraid of the worst label possible - the label of being 'intolerant'. This chapter is not intolerant towards homosexuals, but it does question certain behaviors. Interestingly, men that watch more porn are more approving of same-sex relationships.

A vibrant gay community came to life, resulting in pride parades and all-gay nightclubs. Many homosexuals feel being gay is a strong part of their identity. This makes sense since it is a trait that sets them apart from the majority of the rest of the people. Nonetheless, some take it so far that being gay becomes the one defining aspect of their identity. This is a trait of hypersexuality, where sex is a core part of your identity.

It should also be noted that not all homosexuals frequent these nightclubs, or even attend the pride parades. It is the specific hypersexual element inside the gay community that comes out at these events, and it is this specific subset that we will be discussing here. This subset, whether a minority or majority is unknown, determines the outward culture of the homosexual community. It is this group that appears at the events and refuses to blend into the rest of society. It is this group that turns being gay into a core identity trait, and has an obsession with sex. Our criticism is thus not aimed at homosexuals, but at this homosexual identity. That is because this identity offers a case study of hypersexuality.

Take for example the pride parades. Hundreds, or even thousands of gay men join together to celebrate their gayness and the tolerance towards it. Lesbians join too, but always in far fewer numbers. There is a massive difference between lesbians and homosexuals when it comes to sexuality. Different from porn, real-life lesbians appear to be closer to asexuality.

Men in the parades are dancing around in revealing outfits. They make out with others in public. They wear latex and leather fetish outfits that are made to be worn inside the confines of the bedroom. They expose as much flesh as they can get away with. We can see that there is a strong desire to expose themselves.

Exhibitionism is a hypersexual fetish, it is a sign of having a constant desire to engage in sex. Exposing your body is an invite to others to make use of it, a desperate invite at that. Although in the heterosexual community this used to be looked down upon, it has become more and more accepted and expected for women to dress like streetwalking prostitutes. Especially when they visit a nightclub. How much of that change in clothing is due to the hypersexualization of our society, caused by porn?

At other gay events, men may even come completely naked. One example is the Folsom Street Fair, an annual BDSM event with a strong gay presence in San Francisco. Oral sex and handjobs will be performed in the middle of the street, by complete strangers. Men walk around naked all day, occasionally men will even wear a cockring - a ring that tightly fits around the base of the shaft of the penis to hold the blood there and allow an erection to remain for a longer time. Other activities such as whipping and spanking take place in public stands, they are accessible to the public so that they can watch. Despite the fact that the men coming naked are all sorts of regular, normal homosexuals, most naked women that go there are sex workers; pornstars and prostitutes. What is normal in one subculture, is an outlier in the rest of society.

Some conservative gay voices have wondered if this is the best way to find acceptance in society. Does this behavior really show that gays are just like everybody else? Obviously not, and that is why many homosexual men distance themselves from the homosexual community. They distance themselves from this hypersexual culture that they do not agree with. The question remains whether these dissenting voices are the majority or a minority. The pride parades confirm what the social conservatives have been warning about for decades, namely that gays are sexual deviants and that they will spread this deviancy to the rest of society. Objectively, it is hard to claim that that is not what has happened. Still, it is also hard to attach a moral judgment to this change. Has this change been bad for society, or is it merely a sign of our increased tolerance?

Inside gay nightclubs, there is an excess of alcohol abuse, drug use, and sexual promiscuity. The homosexual community has fully embraced hedonism. The pursuit of fleeting pleasures. Homosexuals can impossibly create a family. The government has blocked gay marriage for a long time. What then is the purpose of sex other than to have fun? What is the value of sex when there can be no offspring? Pregnancy is out of the question, and diseases are accepted as an inconvenient side effect. Sex has become a meaningless pastime, a way to enjoy yourself without any special meaning. No emotional connection is required, comparable to the Tinder-driven hook-up culture in heterosexuals. Tinder, however, was based on the very popular homosexual application called Grindr. The principle is the same, except that Grindr was made purely for homosexuals. Grindr was, and is, extremely popular. It was founded in 2009 by Israeli immigrant Joel Simkhai, after he had moved to the United States. Tinder wasn't launched until 2012, three years later, by two Jewish friends called Justin Mateen and Sean Red.

The popularity of Grindr already shows us that promiscuity is rampant in the gay community. It should be expected that gay men have a very high sexual partner count. It should be expected that many of these men were strangers and casual one-time hookups. These expectations are confirmed when we look at the numbers. In San Francisco half of the gay men had over five hundred different sexual partners. Over a quarter of gay men reported that they had over a thousand sexual partners. More than four out of five gay men reported more than fifty sexual partners. These answers came from men of all ages, including those that were still young. Almost 80% said over half of the men they had sex with were strangers, and 70% said that over half of the men they had sex with was a one-time thing.

Safe sex is often out of the question. They are aware that most diseases can be cured with an antibiotic cure, and many have lost their concern over HIV. Gay men use HIV blockers and medicine is funded by the healthcare system. Frankly, HIV is no longer a death sentence. Besides, the risk of infertility that some STDs bring is no threat to the gay men.

Lifetime sexual partners for straight men and women are generally estimated to average either just below ten, or when taking the higher estimates they will range between ten and twenty. The five hundred was not even a lifetime estimate, it was simply how many partners half of the gay men surveyed had had up to that point in time. Admittedly the survey was done in San Francisco, and perhaps that city attracts a more promiscuous type of homosexual. Still, it is doubtful that location alone would explain the entire difference.

Since straight couples often end up married and are settling down after reaching a certain age and finding their one true love, their partner count stops rising there. Still, even before settling down, even the most promiscuous heterosexuals struggle to reach the numbers obtained by an average homosexual. For homosexuals, such a monogamous phase often simply does not happen and they can continue racking up new partners for many years - and at a much higher pace per year.

Gay men do not value monogamy in the same way as straight couples. Their hypersexual lifestyles are accepting towards promiscuity even within committed relationships. Less than one out of every twenty gay men reported maintaining sexual fidelity within their monogamous relationships. In other words, nineteen out of twenty gay men continue to have sex with other gay men while they are in a relationship. Everything is about sex for them. We see this same feature more and more in heterosexual couples.

A common retort to homosexual promiscuity is that it is the

natural male drive to want to have sex with many people, and to want to have sex more often. It is men that want sex, and women that block them - the women want to build an emotional bond first. To a certain extent this is true, men are naturally less picky about who they have sex with, as they can spread their seed into many wombs, yet women need to protect their womb, because they will carry this man's child inside them for the next nine months. For women, the investment is a lot higher. Regardless, the retort simply does not hold up. Women may be less willing to engage in sex with a new partner, but inside relationships the sexual urges are often equal, sometimes sex is even more desired by the woman. Their libidos do not significantly differ. Thus, the man is left sexually satisfied and we see straight fidelity scores are a lot better than those of gay men. Additionally, a lot of straight men are reluctant to have sex with women they do not know at all. Many prefer to have some sort of emotional connection before going to bed with the other person. The difference between straight and gay men is too large to be explained away by a mere reference to male libido.

Since government-funded medical care pays for the HIV medicines there are no extra costs involved for them. They know that as long as they take their medicines their life expectancy does not change. It is no surprise then that STD infection rates are far higher for homosexuals than anywhere else, especially for syphilis and gonorrhea. These differences in STD infection occurrence are so high that when men go to have an STD test, one of the questions will often be if they have had sex with other men. Only if they answer yes to this question, will they bother to test for syphilis. Otherwise, they feel such a test is an unnecessary waste of resources. Outside of the gay community, this disease is almost non-existent.

There are even stories of gay men called 'bug chasers'. At first sight this appears more like an urban legend, rather than something that actually exists. The internet will show you results and bring you to fora where men are talking about it. What is it that we are talking about here? Bug chasers are men that are looking for HIV-positive men to infect them with the virus. They are chasing their strain of HIV, and consider it their way of sharing something intimate with these men. It could be true if you consider that some men live in constant fear of becoming infected. One way of coping with this fear is to give in; if they are sure they have it, they no longer need to fear the infection. Undoubtedly some readers will at this point have assumed this is an urban legend, so let's read the Wikipedia entry for 'bugchasing'.

''Bugchasing, also known in slang as charging, is the practice of pursuing sexual activity with HIV-positive individuals in order to contract HIV. Individuals engaged in this activity are referred to as bugchasers. It is a form of self-harm. Bugchasers seek sexual partners who are HIV-positive for the purpose of having unprotected sex and becoming HIV-positive; giftgivers are HIV-positive individuals who comply with the bugchasers' efforts to become infected with HIV. Bugchasers indicate various reasons for this activity. Some bugchasers engage in the activity for the excitement and intimacy inherent in pursuing such a dangerous activity, but do not implicitly desire to contract HIV. Some researchers suggest that the behavior may stem from a "resistance to dominant heterosexual norms and mores" due to a defensive response by gay men to repudiate stigmatization and *rejection by society. Some people consider bugchasing "intensely erotic" and the act of being infected through the "fuck of death" as the "ultimate taboo, the most extreme sex act left." People who are HIV negative and in a relationship with someone who is HIV-positive may seek infection as a way to remain in the relationship, particularly when the HIV-positive partner may wish to break up to avoid infecting the HIV negative partner. Others have suggested that some people who feel lonely desire the nurturing community and social services that support people with HIV/AIDS''*

Later on, the article gives an explanation that connects to hypersexuality and sex addiction. Just like porn consumers constantly needing a new rush of adrenaline, so do these men need something new and exciting. They need the most extreme sex act left.

''Dr. David Moskowitz, Dr. Catriona MacLeod and Dr. Michael Roloff attempted to quantitatively explain why bug chasers chase HIV. They claimed that individuals who look for HIV are more likely sex addicts. These individuals have exhausted the sexual high they previously derived by performing other sexual risk taking behaviors, and now turn to bug chasing to achieve the risk-oriented high.''

What is also known is that at some parties HIV-positive men infect other men without them knowing they were infected. In some parts of the world this is a criminal offense, in other parts it has been made legal. California made it a misdemeanor to knowingly infect someone with HIV, and that is punishable by a fine and up to six months in prison, despite the receiver of the disease being marked for life.

Why do we highlight the homosexual hypersexuality so much? Because we can see that it is more and more moving into the same direction for the straight community - at least for certain subsets of the straight population, the ones most perceptible to porn addiction. Moreover, we believe that this move towards promiscuity is fueled not by innate human desire, but excessive porn consumption. That is not to say that all promiscuity is bad and men and women should wait with sex until marriage, but it is possible to take promiscuity so far that it becomes self-destructive behavior that prevents someone from taking care of the rest of their life and putting in effort to achieve other goals.

Biologically, people are in between the chimpanzee and the gorilla. The chimpanzees have many sexual partners and compete mostly with the sperm inside the womb, to see whoever comes to the egg first. Gorillas, on the other hand, control their women and establish a harem, the competition takes place in the world outside where it is determined who gets to mate with the female. Hence the massive amount of muscle that a gorilla has. If you have a harem, you need to be able to defend it. For chimpanzees, everyone gets to mate with everyone. The size of human testes is more similar to those of gorillas. Biologically, humans are in an odd place and compete both in partner selection and in the sperm race towards the egg. This means that some promiscuity among humans is to be expected, but not to the extent that we see it is present in the gay community. They have fully embraced the chimpanzee lifestyle.

Take into account as well that humans often get jealous when thinking that their partner may have sex with someone else. This is a deeply ingrained behavior to demand loyalty. Considering how common jealousy is, especially in the field of relationships, it forms a clear indication that people are naturally more monogamous than chimpanzees. The oxytocin that binds us together during sex is absent in these chimpanzees. It is normal for human couples to bond together and lose interest in others. It is logical when you look at the utter uselessness of a human baby, compared to some of the other animals in the wild. A human baby cannot even crawl the first months of its existence, and only learns to walk years later. Many other animals can walk after mere minutes, which obviously requires less intensive parenting. It is clear that to raise such a baby you need a lot of effort and protection. This is why the couple is needed to raise such a child. For chimpanzees, this necessity is not there, so the father is not necessary to be involved after birth. That is, as long as the father does not harm the child.

How does hypersexuality relate to porn use though? Men that become addicted to porn, are in effect hypersexual. Their mind is spending a huge amount of time thinking about sex, where that sex takes the form of watching pornography. They seek that 'arousal high'. In some cases, this will spill over into real life, where these men will be more likely to engage in risk taking behavior to satisfy their sexual needs. Think about unsafe, condomless, sex with strangers. The risk of pregnancy or STDs is easily ignored. The men may turn to exhibitionism or voyeurism as well. Life, for them, is about chasing their sexual urge. Porn only strengthens their desires, instead of quenching their thirst. They are always looking for something new, a new thrill.

For many straight men, their hypersexual urges cannot always be met by meeting a woman. This problem is much easier for gay men that find a new partner with greater ease. For straight men, their outlet becomes porn. They browse porn not because they want to, but because it forms an outlet for their frustration. They can escape the real world and spend countless hours browsing porn sites, releasing happy hormones in their brain. Porn functions like any other addiction, it is a way to escape reality. However, the more porn they consume, the more porn starts to pull them in, independent of the quality of their real life. Consequently, their life worsens as they do not spend effort on improving it, and porn becomes an even more appealing escape. The vicious cycle of addiction.

Not only is it counterproductive, but it can become truly problematic as a time-sinker. They may be late for meetings, or work, or dates, all because they are unable to separate themselves from their computer or mobile phone. All because they want to watch just one more video. Such sessions where men are jerking off, postponing their orgasm, can last for hours. Porn has made these men addicted to that extreme level of arousal. They may try to chase it desperately in the real world, or, facing rejection from women, indulge in it online. Either way, this can become the dominant focus of their daily lives.

PORN INFLUENCES SOCIETY

Porn is undoubtedly influencing our lives and our world. We have made references to this here and there throughout the book. Sleeping around with multiple people in a casual way has become more accepted. Unsafe sex is frequently tolerated by both sides, ignoring the risks involved. Most effort is taken to prevent pregnancy, often by women taking the pill or other methods of anti-conception. However that does not protect against diseases, only condoms protect against that. However, condoms are not used in porn. How useful is it to ask a new partner if they have an STD or not? More than likely if they would have an STD, they would not be aware of it. Many women can experience STDs without any symptoms. When there are no symptoms, and people have casual sex with varying people within short time spans, diseases can spread easily and unknowingly. Yet people take such chances all the time. Some STDs are already developing resistance to antibiotics. It will be matter of time before a strain with resistance starts spreading globally. Such diseases can lead to infertility, and this was a common result a century ago before antibiotics were introduced. It is not surprising that people were more cautious about sex back then.

Many people don't understand why our society is, or at least used to be, so against promiscuity. Most don't comprehend that it often goes hand in hand with battling against STDs and their severe consequences. One theory even states that humans became monogamous in the past purely to prevent STDs. As people moved into agricultural societies, the risk of STDs increased. While living in a tribe in the woods, the whole tribe may be clean. Nobody has an STD and there is nothing to worry about. However, in the new villages and cities, people from different places all came to live together. If only one had the disease, it could quickly spread through the whole city. These vile cities were a breeding ground for epidemics. Some ancient villages or cities may have evaporated purely due to the widespread consequences of STDs. When all the women become infertile, their sterility will prevent any future generation being born. The places that countered such promiscuity, were the ones that survived.

Even when not the entire village became infected, consequences for those that did get infected would be dire. These STDs would often cause infertility, creating a genetic dead end for those that caught the disease. Those that practiced monogamy came out as the winners, as they were fertile and could have offspring. Monogamy was the Darwinian winner of the evolutionary game. This provides an alternative to the view that monogamy arose to ensure inheritances, although the reality may have been a combination of both. The relevance of inheritance may depend on the societal structure and whether the poor peasants actually have any wealth to pass on as inheritance. The Darwin-effect is present everywhere.

Even today the consequences of STDs are brushed off, including in the sexual education classes. Schools will show how to apply a condom on to a banana, but it ends there. Using a condom, it is implied, you are safe and don't need to worry. Even if you would end up with an STD, a simple visit to the clinic and a week of antibiotics will fix your problems. There's a very casual atmosphere surrounding all of it. There is nothing said of promiscuity, this is all perfectly fine. But many women are not checked regularly and walk around without symptoms for months. Months during which the STD develops inside them, possibly leaving them infertile. Around 10% of women struggle with fertility and conceiving, plus holding onto, a child. It's unknown what percentage of that group has had complications arise due to STDs.

Even look at the way people dress today compared to a mere two decades ago. Nakedness has become more acceptable, even

175

among younger girls. Booty shorts for women have become acceptable, despite the lower half of their asses showing. Boobtubes consist of a tight fabric that stretches around the girl's chest area. Whenever women do wear jeans, they wear skinny jeans that follow the shape and outline of their ass. Worse than skinny jeans are leggings, which have recently become acceptable as a replacement for trousers. Leggings fully follow the outline of the body, leaving nothing hidden. Cleavage is on display at all times.

Women are known to dress more seductively during their ovulation period, when their fertility is highest. This may indicate a certain female-on-female competition for male attention, since they are all eager to receive the highest quality genes. It appears that the widespread display of pornography, nudity and sex has kicked this competitive instinct into overdrive. Women feel they need to compete for male attention at all times. This also confirms that women indeed dress seductively to attract men, despite what some women will tell you.

Regardless of what specific clothes people wear, the overall purpose seems to have moved towards a focus on sex. It has become normal to dress in a way that highlights the shape of your body, rather than to dress with a bit of modesty. We do not wish to pass judgement on girls and women that dress this way, or that the Islamic approach to women's clothing is preferable. Besides, any such a comment is considered 'slut-shaming' behavior nowadays. Humans have shamed wrong behaviors since time immemorial, it is a very effective way to increase cohesion in the community and uphold certain moral values. However, are we not reducing male and female relationships purely to sex? Are we not reducing it to what we see in porn? Women have many qualities, but modern culture appears to emphasize one quality above all. The quality of being sexually attractive to men. Relationships are only about sex, and instead of a relationship starting off with dating and some generic courtship rituals, after which sex takes place - nowadays sex is often what takes place first, out of which a relationship may develop. There are exceptions to this rule, and it must be said that sex is naturally at the core of a relationship. Yet, many other aspects are frequently overlooked. In the past, a relationship was a far more practical union for the purpose of raising the offspring together. With a focus on hedonistic sex and no other kind of match, it is to be expected that this offspring does not arrive and the fertility rates drop.

What are the consequences of the supposed equality of the sexes? Modern thought dictates that men and women are really the same, and that they are capable of the same things. It is a thoughtcrime to say that men are better at certain things than women, although it is perfectly fine to say that women are better at certain things than men. We are made to believe that men and women differ only in their looks, in their sexual traits, and not in other ways. Is that really a beneficial development for women? Feminism does crave equality and all, but is this really an improved situation on what was before? Of course in some ways it is, such as having legal rights equal to those of a man, but we are talking about how men and women work together in a relationship here. Women can improve the life of a man in many ways, but since everything had to be made equal, now the only thing that is added is sex.

What we mean is that before a woman would want to be a mother. She would cook, clean and care for the household. She would bring warmth and kindness, turn the house into a home. The man would provide financial stability and protection. But what when these tasks are made equal? In fairness, it is arguable as to how much the male tasks have been equalized. The man is still the primary financial source, as women have little interest in men that earn less money than them. They do not respect men that earn less, there is nothing to admire in the man when the women earn more on their own. The same often goes for fixes around the home, taking care of the garden, fixing the car and all and any other traditional male task around the house. When women do still perform their traditional role, it is looked down upon by feminists.

Those women are considered to be oppressed by the patriarchy.

The woman works, or receives government benefits, and no longer needs a man for financial stability. The world is safe, at least in large parts of the Western world where feminism has most severely taken hold, so protection is not required. Since the defeat of Adolf Hitler, the Western world has seen peace. War is a thing of history and distant countries. Murders and extreme violence are relatively rare compared to any other moment in history, and largely restricted to specific areas. Rape culture is present in other parts of the world, but not in the West. At least, when adhering to the general definition of rape, instead of expanding it to include all women that changed their mind about sex later on. This part of the world is so safe, that women have forgotten how brutal the world can be. They have forgotten that men can offer protection, or that such protection may be needed. Any required sense of security is provided by the government, who has taken over the role of father of the family, and husband to the adult women.

At the same time, women insist that men take an equal part in the responsibilities around the household. Men should cook, clean and support in raising the children. Many women, especially the ones more supportive of feminism, even feel like it is not their responsibility to bring warmth and compassion. Such feminists have taken on a very entitled attitude, but are overall a minority in the total group of women. Most women naturally gravitate towards their biological tendencies, and the same can be said for men. Our instincts keep society in order, but that does not prevent small influential groups trying to change it. A combination of stress at work and a desire to be equal to men have left these women in constant competition for control. The corporate world has always been male dominated, and women that wish to succeed often try to mimic male behavior in order to succeed. This unnatural behavior is more draining for them, than for the men around them. This unnatural state of equality takes continuous effort and strain. Within the relationship, it pushes the women into conflicts of control with the husband. Since they are equal in all ways, there is only one aspect left where the man and woman add value to each other's lives. Sex. Here, in this most basic instinct, in the heat of the moment, nature takes control. The men are dominant and the women are submissive. This one place where they take on their natural roles is where they truly feel liberated. This is what they desire and find so hard to achieve in the outside world.

We should add and amplify that this does not apply to the full amount of the citizens. Many women bring warmth and many men offer protection and stability. Yet, such relationships are in the modern world immediately considered to be traditional and old-fashioned. Women that take part in such relationships are said to be not true feminists, as such relationships based on conservative morals can only be the result of the dominance of patriarchy. Or so they say.

We mentioned before that men consider porn a good enough substitute for a relationship and dealing with actual women. It is no wonder when we consider that sex is really the only thing that is added to their lives. Or better said, the only aspect they recognize as a value adding activity. Unless a man has a strong desire to have children, there isn't much need for a woman beyond sex. And for that animalistic purpose, he can never find a woman as good as the girls he watches in porn videos. Even if they would be as good, he would soon get bored and desire some novelty, as that is what he is used to. To the porn addict, a real woman can no longer compete to the ones on his screen. She does not appeal to him any longer, the man's mind has been infected with the porn virus.

Our sex acts change as well. Anal sex has become a standard part of sex for many couples, despite the damage brought on to the anus. Especially odd is when men not only like, but prefer anal sex. It lacks the natural lubrication and smoothness of the vagina. Not to mention that you may encounter bits and pieces of feces when inserting your penis into someone else's rectum. Several reasons may be provided for the rise in anal sex.

The first is that for men with a small penis, the tighter opening may supply them with a sensation they can not receive in the relatively loose vagina. The looseness of the vagina depends on the girl, but men that lack girth may not feel the same pressure in the vagina as in the ass. For those with a normal or above average sized penis, anal sex probably creates more problems with fitting it in properly than that it provides pleasure. Especially if a girl is not used to receiving anal, it would require a certain delicacy. This would not be a problem for those that have received anal so often, that their anus has become looser. However, when that is the case, it more or less defeats the whole point of anal in the first place. You will be able to tell if an anus has received a lot of sex just by looking at it.

A second option is that men seek to dominate their women. They can no longer be the first to have sex with them, but perhaps they can be the first to have anal sex with them. Or, if they cannot even be the first to have anal sex with a girl, then he should at least compare to the other man that she did allow to perform anal on her. It would be humiliating if the girl you are dating allowed another man to do something sexually, but she will not allow you to do the same. It would indicate that the sex with the other man was more special, or more valued to her, than sex with her newest partner. Some men would perceive it that way, and perhaps there is some truth to that.

The last and most likely option. The only option that describes a plausible explanation for all men and women. Both men and women have seen so much porn that they have started to believe anal sex is perfectly normal. Any time you open a pornsite you will see videos of women receiving anal, it is almost more common than just regular vaginal intercourse. Consuming this for hours on end, the newest generation has the belief that anal is nothing special. Similar to changing positions during sex, so too do they vary the hole that gets penetrated. When people think of porn when they think of sex, any act that is normal in porn will become normalized in their own bedrooms. No porn consumer is immune to these levels of propaganda that they voluntarily consume.

But other, more specific fetishes, are more and more common as well. As is the use of sexual toys used in masturbation for both men and women. Cuckoldry. Sex in public. Exhibitionism. The fetishization of the black man. Sex involving more than two people. Everything that is normalized in porn, becomes normalized in real sex. Such is the power of mass consumption.

To briefly continue about anal porn, let's digress a little here. Anal porn is also ultimately about submission and a degree of humiliation. Several years, or decades, ago, anal was not a very common activity between men and women. Sodomy was forbidden by the bible and it was primarily gay men that resorted to this option due to a lack of other options available to them. For the women, it would often hurt more than it would bring pleasure. Although, it can still bring pleasure to women - partially due to applying pressure to the right regions and partially due to the joy they get from their submission. Nonetheless, in porn, gay and straight culture are brought together and suddenly anal scenes became a lot more common. Almost every video includes some anal sex, and there are even the highly unhygienic 'ass to mouth' scenes where the anal sex is followed with a blowjob. That is one way to make sure you end up with an infection later on, you might as well eat poop.

Currently, boyfriends everywhere try to convince their girlfriends to do anal. Girls are seen as prudish when they refuse, and they are pressured into it against their will by men on a whole relentlessly pushing them for it. It is simply another example of how porn culture invades our real sexual culture. Men push for it, they demand it, and even expect it, because porn has shown them that it is a normal element of sex. In their minds, not having anal sex means something normal is missing. Girls don't push back much, or are curious themselves, as their minds are often also influenced by porn.

"Essentially it comes from every man who is unhappily married, and he looks at his wife who just nagged at him about this or that or what not and he says, 'I'd like to **** you in the ***.' He's angry at her, right? And he can't, so he would rather watch some girl taking it **** and fantasize at that point he's doing whatever girl happened to be mean to him that particular day, and that is the attraction, because when people watch anal, nobody wants to watch a girl enjoying anal."

- Paul Hesky

The same applies to threesomes, making a sex tape, using all sorts of sex toys. All these things are normalized by people watching porn. Their views on sex are heavily influenced by porn, more than anyone wants to admit. Since people start to view porn at such a young age, it becomes difficult to tell what a normal sexual activity would look like. People around the world are trying to recreate what they see in porn. They feel incompetent when they cannot reach the same spectacular results and fireworks.

Society as a whole has been moving towards more extreme forms of porn. All sorts of fetish videos are on the rise as the world is getting desensitized to the more 'vanilla' type of internet porn. More violent, more humiliating porn is all on the rise.

*"People want more. They want to know how many **** you can shove up an ***... It's like Fear Factor meets Jackass. Make it more hard, make it more nasty, make it more relentless. The guys make the difference. You need a good guy, who's been around and can give a good scene, **** 'em hard. I did my homework. These guys are intense."*

- Mitchell Spinelli

If Playboy would have been launched today, people would not even find it stimulating. Simple pictures of naked women; these no longer hold enough appeal to a generation of men that are accustomed to internet porn. Worse even, the Playboy magazine was released monthly. One new girl to look at every month? Men nowadays click to see a new video every five seconds. Simply opening up the main page of a porn site shows them more than a year subscription on Playboy would. And all of that in the blink of an eye, for free, in full anonymity.

So what do people search for? Anal, teen, MILF are some of the top searches. So is ebony, latina and Japanese. Now the Japanese have an odd interest in porn, coming up with the vilest sort imaginable. From news anchors being molested, to weird incest-provoking game shows, all the way to tentacle porn. All of it with blurred out genitals, as Japanese law requires some censorship. The censorship does not prevent them from creating porn that would be disgusting to a normal person. Equally odd is the top position for searches for Hentai and cartoon porn. This porn doesn't even involve real women anymore, it's all animated cartoonery. When sex equals porn in your mind, it matters little whether the women are real or not. Touching them isn't an option anyway.

These are only some of the biggest global searches, not all the niches and fetishes different people are looking for. If we go into that, we can see that things like menstruation porn, or milking porn are on the rise. Yes, milking porn is the sexualization of lactating mothers. We see that on a global level we are getting desensitized to porn, looking for stranger videos. Moreover, the porn industry eagerly complies and creates this strange material. Since there is so much free porn already available online, it is in these niches that they can still earn some money. In order to give that same arousal high, porn needs to shock and bring something new, something that these veteran porn addicts have never seen before. They need this shock to wake up their desensitized minds.

Not only do we look for more extreme material. The more extreme material also finds us with greater ease. The odd varieties of porn leak into the main page or into related videos, so that even people that don't go out searching for them will stumble upon them. Besides, every category of porn gets more extreme. Porn becomes more violent, both verbally and physically. Bondage and the like become a part of an average browsing session. And all of that weirdness leaks back into mainstream society, slowly and without people really noticing.

THE MEANING OF MASCULINITY

''Masculinity is not something that is given to you, but something you gain. And you gain it by winning small battles with honor.''

- Norman Mailer

Manliness, masculinity, virility. All three words refer to more or less the same thing.

For manliness we find: "The traditional male quality of being brave and strong."

For masculinity we find: "Qualities or attributes regarded as characteristic of men. 'handsome, muscled, and driven, he's a prime example of masculinity'"

For virility we find: "(in a man) the quality of having strength, energy, and a strong sex drive; manliness. 'great importance is placed on a man's virility'"

Since the root 'vir' in virility comes from the Latin and means 'man', we see that all these words are in fact synonyms. The same goes for the word virtue. In modern days the terms masculinity and manliness have replaced virility as it has gone out of fashion. With that, it has also lost some of its meaning. So far what we can take from these definitions is that men are apparently brave, strong, muscled and driven with a lot of energy.

In the past a man with virility was a man that showed he possessed virilitas. What was it that the ancient Romans meant with this term? It was not only about sexual prowess, although it did not exclude it either. The term was bigger, more encompassing than that. A man needed to be steadfast and assertive. A man needed to be in shape and expand his physique in the gymnasium. A man needed to procreate, and sire offspring. A man needed to have intellectual pursuits. He needed to be calm and resolute. Simultaneously, he needed to be vigorous and courageous. Yet, in all cases knowing his own limits. Together this forms a sort of stoic Renaissance man. All of these characteristics continue to shape our idea of what a man is. A perfect man that possesses and has mastered all these qualities may not exist, but that is no reason to say that not all men should aim to achieve these virtues. A man with virility lives a virtuous life of accomplishment, not a hedonistic life filled with vices.

Such ambitions are what drives society forward. Society is no more than a group of individuals. It relies on the strength of every individual to grow and move towards greater prosperity and grander achievements. It relies on virtuous adult men, for it is their combined will that exerts itself in the form of the state. Throughout history, the world has been shaped by men with courage and self-confidence. Never by men that seclude themselves from society to watch naked women and jerk off to them.

The Romans had one core trait that was absolutely required for any virile man. The trait of self-control. A man was expected to stay level-headed and in control of his emotions. The man is the proverbial rock that provides steadiness. A virile man is grounded, always making sure the ship stays on course. Following the tradition of stoicism, a man should not constantly give in to his base desires. The hot-headed 'macho' men depicted in the movies are a poor Hollywood-depiction of what manliness is. Those men are controlled by their emotions, and thereby lacking virtue and virility. Masculinity is about more than muscle, though it definitely contains muscle. The muscle is not there to be broadcast at any unsuited moment, but to show the other that you could. It can be compared to countries having standing armies and nuclear weapons. Countries do not possess a nuclear arsenal for the sake of throwing it around in a tantrum, but to show other countries their military might and that if they so decided that they would have the option to use them. Men should have an imposing physique for the same purpose. Similarly, men are not supposed to give in too often to the charms of women, for it shows a lack of self control. No virile man starts to drool every time a picture of an attractive woman appears on their screen. No man would be unable to resist the urge to masturbate to porn. No, these masculine men would not allow themselves to be distracted by such nonsense, and instead focus on bettering themselves and their environment.

''*The most gentle people in the world are macho males. People who are confident in their masculinity and have a feeling of well-being in themselves. They don't have to kick in doors, mistreat women, or make fun of gays.*''

- Clint Eastwood

It is not masculinity that is at the core of today's 'toxic masculinity' and supposed crisis around the male identity. It is quite the opposite, a lack of virility. Men are led by their desires and emotions, instead of following virtue. When men are confident and content, they do not rape. Such men would not abuse or harass women.

Yet men today, both young and old, have no guidance any longer on how to attain such virility. They are not raised with an ideal of what makes a good man. Instead, they are repeatedly told that they have evil tendencies in them, merely for being men. The answer becomes to be in touch with their emotional feminine side, but it is this misguided reply that leads to anger outbursts and killing sprees.

What then, is the effect of porn? Throughout this book the attempt has been to explain the effects of pornography on the male mind. This was done by observing why certain types of porn are appealing, highlighting the trend of men becoming submissive. Porn makes men weak and insecure, rather than confident and strong. It is a force of destruction on society, for all that are involved. The only winners are the owners of the porn industry, as they rake in the money. They are a combination of pimps and dealers, as they whore out the women in their labor force to acquire currency from the countless addicts around the world. All of us, are inclined to be porn addicts, because all men have a natural sex drive. Porn triggers those parts of our reptile brain, and fools us. And that is exactly where this virility and self-control is needed. We are not animals, we can rise above our instincts. We can think rationally and be in control of our passions, instead of allowing our passions to control us. There is no greater obstacle that stands in the way of men achieving their goals and dreams, than porn. A Christian could rightfully call it the work of Satan, a Zoroastrian and Star Wars fan alike would refer to it as the dark side. Whatever you wish to call it, remember that it is poison to your mind, and if you believe we possess one, to the soul.

Porn is not harmful because it increases masculinity. One, because it really does not increase masculinity. Two, because our problem is not with too much masculinity. Porn is harmful for another reason. Our problem is that porn turns men into submissive addicts that don't take control over their lives and refuse to lead. They lead lives of vice, or better put, it is vice that leads their lives. Men become meek, weak and vigorless. They waste their days without purpose, enslaved to their hedonistic desires.

What is missing is virility, a way of living that gives men purpose, a reason to live. Virility is the cure for nihilism, it is what every adolescent man secretly desires. To broadcast their virilitas, this is why men exist, and it something men will need to do once more. It provides satisfaction. It counters depression. It appeals women. It turns the masturbatory porn consumption and casual sex into healthy relationships based on affection, followed by procreation. Our current toxic lack of manliness drives men and women apart, their equality pushes them away from one another. It is virility that has the power to unite men and women and solve our problems.

The problem our world faces is a lack of virility, and the cause is porn.

AFTERWORD

Perhaps this book has been able to teach you matters you did not know before. Any dubious statement on fact mentioned in this book, can be easily found with a brief search on Google, Yahoo, or Bing. References to evolutionary psychology are still relevant, despite being more frequently attacked in recent times by those that wish to deny our ancestry.

Most of all, this book may be helpful for some to end their endless consumption of porn and move towards a more productive and fulfilling life.

Printed in Great Britain
by Amazon

84888392R00114